IDE

TREES
of Britain and Ireland

Bob Press

Photographic Consultant

Bob Gibbons

HarperCollins*Publishers*

HarperCollins*Publishers*
London · Glasgow · New York · Sydney
Auckland · Toronto · Johannesburg

First published 1996

Other titles in the Wild Guide series

Birds of Britain and Ireland

Flowers of Britain and Ireland

Butterflies and Moths of Britain and Europe

Mushrooms and Toadstools of Britain and Europe

Title page photograph: Oak leaves, *Quercus* × *pseudosuber*

Artwork by Carol Merryman

All pictures supplied by Natural Image. The copyright in the photographs belongs to Bob Gibbons apart from the following: Robin Fletcher 19, 22, 24, 37, 41, 48, 100, 146, 170, 179; Nature Photographers 101 (Frank V Blackburn), 167 (Brinsley Burbidge), 90 (Andrew Cleave); Peter Wilson 42, 60, 79, 80, 86, 88, 129, 161, 162, 176.

ISBN 0 00 220009 0

Edited and designed by D & N Publishing, Ramsbury, Wiltshire
Colour reproduction by Colourscan, Singapore
Printed and bound by Rotolito Lombarda Spa, Milan, Italy

PREFACE

Trees are so familiar and commonplace that we often take them for granted. It is usually only when great changes affect the tree population, such as the aftermath of major storms or the rapid loss of thousands of trees from disease, that we realise what a major element they are in the world around us. In fact, few people live in entirely treeless surroundings, even in towns and cities, and trees have an important influence on everyday living, whether directly or indirectly.

Trees perform a number of vital functions in the environment. Like all green plants, they are able to use the energy of sunlight to manufacture basic foods, such as sugars, on which all life depends. As part of this process, they also help maintain the level of oxygen in the atmosphere. Trees play a significant rôle in preventing the erosion of soil by binding it with their roots, and their dead leaves greatly improve soil fertility when they rot to form humus. They also provide habitats for other wildlife, both animals and other plants, which rely on trees for food and shelter. Humans have always relied heavily on trees and many species have important commercial uses. As well as timber for fuel and building, they yield food and drink, forage for domestic stock and a variety of other products ranging from cork, paper pulp, matches, dyes and tanning agents to perfumes, medicines, gums and even jewellery. Nowadays, there is a large industry based solely on the use of trees as ornamental and amenity plants to delight the eye and improve the quality of our own, man-made, habitat.

HOW TO USE THIS BOOK

This book covers 176 species of trees, including all those commonly found in the wild in the British Isles, as well as those frequently planted in streets and public parks and gardens.

Each page of the main section of the book has a **photograph** of a tree, and an illustration showing additional details. The common name of the tree is given, together with its scientific name and the name of the plant family to which it belongs. At the top of the page is a leaf **symbol**. The leaf outline indicates the family to which the tree belongs. It will help you to see which trees are related to each other and can be used as a quick guide when identifying a tree since the general shape is typical for each family. There are exceptions to this rule, so the symbol is meant as a guide only. The colour of the symbol is used to distinguish different families and does not indicate the true colour of the leaves. Adjacent to each symbol is an indication of the tree's height and whether it is evergreen or deciduous. The lighter portion of the **calendar bar** indicates those months in which you will usually find this tree in flower. For conifers the lighter portion indicates when the tree is shedding pollen from male cones (where this information is not available the calendar bar has been omitted). Again, this is meant only as a guide. Flowering can be brought forward or delayed by several weeks, depending on the seasonal weather conditions. It can also be affected by geography – as a general rule flowering is delayed for trees growing further north.

The **ID Fact File** lists features that will help you to identify each species and the general text provides further information. The names of any similar trees are listed at the end of the ID Fact File.

To identify a tree, look through the book to find the most likely match. The leaf symbols will help. Remember, if you know, to check if the tree is evergreen or deciduous. Use the ID Fact File to see if the description matches the tree. If it does not, check any similar species listed, as well as those trees described on adjacent pages. The species are arranged in order of their closest relationships, so the tree you are trying to identify should be nearby.

HISTORY OF TREES IN EUROPE

In geological terms, the modern history of trees in Europe dates from the last Ice Age, when the advance of glaciers caused huge changes in the distribution patterns across the continent. As the glaciers retreated, some trees were able to recolonise or even expand their former territory; others remained only in the warmer southern boundaries of the continent or were left as isolated populations in high mountains by the retreating ice.

At the end of the Ice Age several forest types became established across Europe. In the coldest and most exposed parts of the far north where trees are able to survive, the forests are mainly of birches and larches. The remainder of the cold northern regions are occupied by boreal forest, composed of narrow-leaved, evergreen conifers. Broad-leaved deciduous forests form a wide band across the middle of Europe, from the western coasts and Britain to central eastern Europe. This is mainly mixed woodland dominated by oaks on the deeper, wetter soils and beeches on drier, lighter ones. A second type of broad-leaved forest, but an evergreen one, was found in southern Europe, around the shores of the Mediterranean Sea. Composed of species such as Evergreen Oaks and Olives, it has been almost entirely destroyed. Other forest types occupy much smaller areas with specific growing conditions. Willows and alders, for example, dominate in very wet areas.

Although the large tracts of natural forest have been greatly reduced by human activity and some species are now rare, man's introduction of numerous trees from other parts of the world means that the variety of trees now present in Europe is greater than ever before. Introduced trees may be grown in large-scale plantations or confined to streets, parks or gardens. A few have escaped into the wild, becoming established and fully naturalised in different parts of Europe. These introductions began so long ago that the precise origins of some species are unknown and the process is still occurring, so the number of trees to be seen in Europe will continue to increase.

WHAT IS A TREE?

Trees are woody plants which have a single, well-developed main stem or trunk which branches well above ground level, usually at a height of 2 m or more. The trunk and main branches are covered with a protective layer of bark. These are the only features which all trees have in common as trees do not belong to a single group of plants but are found in many different and unrelated plant families.

The division between shrubs and trees is rather blurred. Shrubs are also woody plants but are generally smaller, with several stems which branch at or near ground level. All of the species in this book will form trees where conditions are appropriate.

Unlike non-woody plants, trees grow in both height and girth each year. The increase in height is achieved simply by the elongation of the branches. The increase in girth is achieved by the addition of an extra layer of woody tissue on the trunk and branches. These layers can be seen as the annual rings exposed when a tree is felled.

Trees are often divided into evergreen and deciduous species. **Evergreens** shed and replace their leaves gradually over a period of years. The leaves are often leathery or waxy to reduce water loss or withstand the cold, so evergreens are typical of cold or mountainous regions, but are also common in hot, dry habitats. **Deciduous** trees shed all of their leaves each year, and remain bare through the winter. This allows the trees to remain dormant, husbanding their resources during the harshest season. Their leaves are generally thinner and more delicate than those of evergreens and are more prone to wilting and frost damage.

Many trees reproduce by means of **flowers**, and the fruits and seeds which develop later. Those species which are wind pollinated often have tiny flowers, lacking sepals and petals; and the flowers appear well before the leaves in spring. Insect-pollinated trees have larger, more showy flowers, which are often produced later in the year. One large group of trees which does not have flowers is the conifers, so-called because of their cone-shaped reproductive organs.

GLOSSARY

Alternate With leaves scattered along the twig.
Anther Fertile tip of a stamen, containing pollen.
Bract Leaf-like structure at base of leaf or cone scale.
Capsule Dry fruit usually splitting when ripe to release seeds.
Catkin Slender spike of tiny flowers usually lacking sepals and petals, and wind pollinated.
Cultivar Plant bred by gardeners, not occurring naturally in the wild.
Involucre Leaf-like structure, usually green or greenish, surrounding flowers and fruits.
Leaflet Separate division of a leaf.
Native Originating from an area.
Naturalised Fully established in the wild in areas outside original distribution.
Opposite With leaves arranged in pairs along the twig.
Ovary Female part of a flower containing egg cells and, eventually, seeds.
Pinnate Divided into two rows of leaflets along a central axis.
Palmate Divided into leaves which spread from a single point like fingers of a hand.
Semi-evergreen Retaining most leaves in all except the harshest conditions.
Stamen Male part of a flower consisting of a slender stalk bearing the pollen sacks or anthers.
Stipule Small, leaf-like structure at the base of the leaf-stalk.
Style Usually a slender organ on top of the ovary bearing a surface receptive to pollen.
Sucker New shoot growing from the roots of a tree.
Twice pinnate With each of the pinnate divisions themselves pinnately divided.
Trifoliate With three leaflets.

IDENTIFYING TREES

All plants have specific characteristics, or combinations of characteristics, which enable them to be identified, even among species that have a similar overall appearance. Not all features are equally useful or even constant. Plants on rich soils, for example, tend to produce lush growth and may have larger leaves than plants of the same species growing on poor soils. Identifying trees can be more difficult than identifying herbaceous plants simply because the necessary parts are often out of reach and cannot be observed easily. However, with practise, identification can become quite easy. Always examine the tree and its parts closely and be sure you are comparing similar structures and not, for example, mistaking a stipule for a leaflet. The different parts of a tree and the characters they provide are described here as an initial guide to recognition.

The **height** of a tree varies considerably with age, soil depth, exposure and other environmental factors. The heights given in this book are the maximum normally attained by each species; many individual trees will be smaller. The **crown** of the tree is made up of the branches and twigs. The outline or overall shape is often distinctive although it can vary with age. There may be a recognisable **pattern of branching** and the branches themselves may be arched or pendulous. Conifers often have branches in regular whorls which may clothe the trunk almost to the ground. Most non-coniferous trees have rather irregular branching patterns. **Twigs** can be hairy or coloured. These characters generally occur only on young growth as hairs are lost with age and older twigs become duller and darker. The presence or absence of spines on the twigs is also a useful distinguishing feature. The **trunk** provides few useful characters other than general features such as being short, stout or bare for most of its length.

Bark is less useful than is often supposed for identifying trees but the overall colour, texture and whether the bark sheds in strips or flakes provide some clues. The texture varies with age to some extent, usually becoming rougher and often more cracked and fissured in old trees. Sometimes the outer layers of bark peel or flake to reveal brighter layers beneath.

Leaves are a major source of identification characters. Start by looking at their arrangement on the twigs: for example, are they alternate (scattered along the twig) or opposite? Are the leaves pinnately (with two rows of leaflets arranged along the central axis) or palmately divided (with leaflets spreading like fingers of a hand)? Are the leaves or leaflets lobed, toothed, or entire? All of these features are relatively constant and reliable. The size of the leaves is also important but spans a range rather than being a precise measurement as it can vary somewhat with age and growing conditions. Other useful features may include texture (whether thin or leathery), colour (often different when unfolding in spring and frequently so in autumn), degree of hairiness and the distribution of hairs on the leaf. Leaves are generally paler and more hairy on the underside than on their upper surface. **Stipules** are small, leaf-like organs which occur at the base of the leaf-stalk in some species.

Flowers and **fruits** are also important. Look at the size and shape of the flowers. Are petals present and if so, how many are there and are they of equal size? The way in which the flowers are arranged is often a useful character, for example in spikes or clusters, or scattered singly along the twigs? Also note whether the flowers are borne on new wood, that is the current year's growth, or on old wood which is the lower, thicker parts of the twigs. Many trees have single-sexed flowers: male flowers have only stamens while female ones have an ovary and style but no stamens.

The type of fruit (fleshy, berry-like, dry), together with its size and colour when ripe, also provides clues to identity. Only trees with hermaphrodite or female flowers bear fruit.

One group of trees, the **conifers**, bears cones instead of flowers and fruits. It includes firs, pines and spruces. The pollen-bearing male cones are usually small and sometimes brightly coloured. Female cones are larger, and the scales which make up the cone become woody as the seeds ripen. The shape and arrangement of the cone scales are important characteristics.

WHAT NEXT?

For those who want to take their interest in trees further, there are organisations at all levels in the British Isles that welcome new members. Some cover all plant groups, others concentrate on trees, but all offer opportunities to learn more about identifying, appreciating and conserving trees. As well as the few organisations listed here, there are many local natural history societies and field clubs throughout Britain and Ireland.

The Botanical Society for the British Isles is for amateur and professional botanists interested in British plantlife.
The National Trust owns and manages many gardens containing fine collections of trees.
The Royal Society for the Conservation of Nature co-ordinates the network of County Naturalists and Wildlife Trusts in Britain and Northern Ireland.
The Royal Forestry Society of England, Wales and Northern Ireland caters for members of all levels with an interest in trees, woodland and forest.
The Tree Council promotes knowledge about trees and their care and acts as a forum for other organisations.
The Woodland Trust acts to protect and re-establish areas of broad-leaved woodland.

There is a wide variety of books to take you further in your study of trees. Useful references include:
Trees and Shrubs Hardy in the British Isles by WJ Bean (1970–88).
Woodlands to Visit in England and Wales by The Forestry Trust (1995).
Willows and Poplars of Great Britain and Northern Ireland by RD Meikle (1984).
Shrubs by R Phillips and M Rix (1989).
Field Guide to the Trees of Britain and Northern Europe by JR Press (1992).
Trees and Woodland in the British Landscape by Oliver Rackham (1990).
Bark: the Formation, Characteristics and Uses of Bark Around the World by KB Sandved, GT Prance and AE Prance (1993).

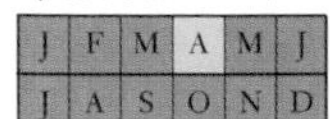

Common Silver Fir

Abies alba

ID FACT FILE

Crown:
Narrowly conical to pyramidal

Bark:
Greyish, cracked

Leaves:
Flattened needles 15–30 mm, blue-green with 2 silvery bands beneath; spreading to form a parting on upper side of shoot

Cones:
10–20 cm, cylindrical, erect. Each scale has a deflexed bract beneath

Large natural forests of Common Silver Fir extend across Europe from N Spain eastwards to the Balkan Peninsula. This species was also extensively planted for timber in other areas such as Britain but it has a low resistance to pollution, pests and frosts. Other, hardier, species are preferred nowadays and Common Silver Fir is less commonly grown than previously.

Evergreen
Up to 70 m

J	F	M	A	M	J
J	A	S	O	N	D

Caucasian Fir

Abies nordmanniana

ID FACT FILE

CROWN: Pyramidal; branched almost from ground level

BARK: Greyish, cracked

LEAVES: Flattened needles 15–30 mm, blue-green with 2 silvery bands beneath; all curved up and forwards around shoot

CONES: 10–20 cm, cylindrical, erect. Each scale has a long, deflexed bract beneath

A native of the Caucasus mountains and upland parts of N Turkey, this species is similar to the closely related Common Silver Fir and is also widely planted as a timber tree. It is usually taller than its relative, with a broader, more densely branched crown. The trees often retain all of their branches so the crown extends down almost to ground level, even in old trees.

Evergreen
Up to 100 m

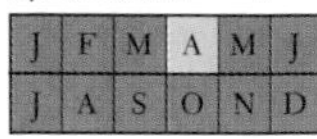

Grand Fir

Abies grandis

ID FACT FILE

CROWN:
Narrowly conical

BARK:
Brown; young twigs olive-green

LEAVES:
Flattened needles 20–60 mm, dark green with 2 silvery bands beneath, aromatic; spreading to leave a central parting along shoot

CONES:
5–10 cm, erect, cylindrical, tapering towards blunt tip. Bracts not visible beneath scales

The stately Grand Fir is native to western N America and is widely grown in N and central Europe. One of the tallest of the Firs, it is a fast-growing tree reaching heights of up to 100 m in its native regions. Trees in Europe are smaller but most are still growing and have yet to reach their full size. The tree's resistance to disease makes it a valuable timber species but it is just as frequently planted as an ornamental tree.

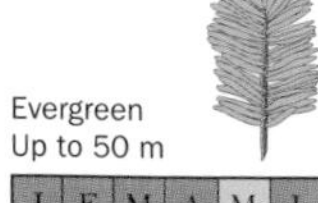

Evergreen
Up to 50 m

J	F	M	A	M	J
J	A	S	O	N	D

Noble Fir

Abies procera

ID FACT FILE

CROWN:
Narrowly conical. Young twigs reddish-hairy

BARK:
Pale grey, smooth; trunk stout

LEAVES:
Flattened, blunt needles 10–35 mm, bluish-green; curved upwards to leave a parting on lower side of shoot

CONES:
12–20 cm, erect, cylindrical. Long, deflexed bract beneath each scale gives cone a shaggy look

The very large scales with long, down-turned bracts are characteristic of Noble Fir. Seeds often germinate in large numbers on fallen and decaying trees, forming rows along the trunks. Noble Fir originates from the coastal mountains of western N America where it is mostly found on the wetter, west-facing slopes. It is often planted in N and W Europe where it thrives on poor soils.

Evergreen
Up to 65 m

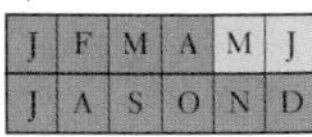

Norway Spruce

Picea abies subsp. *abies*

ID FACT FILE

Crown:
Conical

Bark:
Reddish-brown, smooth at first, becoming finely cracked

Leaves:
Narrow, 4-sided needles, 10–25 mm, stiff, sharp-pointed, dark green; spreading to reveal lower side of shoot; persistent peg-like bases

Cones:
10–18 cm, erect and dark red at first but red-brown and pendulous when mature. Cone scales have squarish or notched tips

Norway Spruce is a major forest tree throughout much of N Europe and in mountains as far south as the Alps and the Balkan Peninsula. It is also planted for timber and to provide shelter. In Britain and elsewhere it is perhaps most familiar as the Christmas tree; many young trees are grown each year specifically for this purpose.

Evergreen
10–12 m

Brewer's Weeping Spruce

Picea breweriana

ID FACT FILE

CROWN:
Pyramidal. Branches spreading, foliage weeping

BARK:
Scaly, streaked with pink and purple

LEAVES:
Flattened but fleshy needles, 20–35 mm, stiff, curved; dark bluish-green with 2 white bands beneath; radiating all around shoot; persistent, peg-like bases

CONES:
10–12 cm, cylindrical, narrow, purple becoming brown and pendulous when mature. Scales rounded

Brewer's Weeping Spruce is a slender, graceful tree widely planted in parks and gardens. Its weeping habit, with both the smaller shoots and the dark green foliage hanging down from the curving main branches, is unusual among conifers and gives a decorative appearance as well as making this species easy to recognise. It is a slow-growing tree native only to the mountains of California and Oregon in the western USA.

Evergreen
Up to 60 m

J	F	M	A	M	J
J	A	S	O	N	D

Sitka Spruce

Picea sitchensis

ID FACT FILE

Crown:
Conical, with a stout trunk

Bark:
Grey, scaly and peeling

Leaves:
Flattened needles, 15–30 mm, stiff, pointed, dark green with 2 bluish-white bands beneath. In older growth upper needles are pressed to shoot, lower spread to form a parting beneath shoot. Persistent, peg-like bases

Cones:
6–10 cm, cigar-shaped, blunt, pendulous when mature. Scales diamond-shaped

This is the tallest of the Spruces and is capable of growing at rates of up to 1 m per year. Since it can achieve such growth even on wet and poor soils it is widely grown as a timber tree and is planted on a large scale in NW and central Europe. A N American species, Sitka Spruce takes its name from Sitka Island in Alaska but occurs as far south as California.

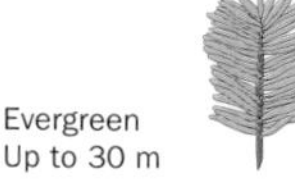

Evergreen
Up to 30 m

Colorado Spruce

Picea pungens

ID FACT FILE

Crown:
Conical with regular whorls of horizontal branches

Bark:
Dark brown, scaly

Leaves:
Needles 20–30 mm, 4-sided, very stiff, prickly, grey- or sometimes blue-green; radiating all around shoot and pointing forwards; persistent, peg-like bases

Cones:
6–10 cm, broadly cylindrical, pendulous when mature. Scales tapering to narrow, blunt and slightly ragged tips

As the name suggests, Colorado Spruce comes from the southwestern part of the USA, including the state of Colorado. The normal form usually has grey-green or bluish leaves and is sometimes planted for timber. Another form, in which the leaves are an intense blue-green colour and which is often called the Blue Spruce, is more commonly seen as an ornamental tree in parks and gardens.

Evergreen
Up to 50 m

J	F	M	A	M	J
J	A	S	O	N	D

Engelmann's Spruce

Picea engelmannii

Engelmann's Spruce has bluish leaves resembling those of the blue form of Colorado Spruce. The wild form of Engelmann's Spruce which is native to the Rocky Mountains of N America, is sometimes planted for timber in Europe and has foliage which smells unpleasant when crushed. The form usually planted in parks in Europe has foliage which smells pleasantly of menthol.

ID FACT FILE

Crown:
Conical

Bark:
Brown, scaly

Leaves:
Needles 15–25 mm, 4-sided, soft, bluish-green, smelling of menthol when crushed; spreading to form a parting beneath shoot; persistent, peg-like bases

Cones:
3.5–7.5 cm, cylindrical, pendulous when mature. Scales squarish, tips ragged

Evergreen
Up to 30 m

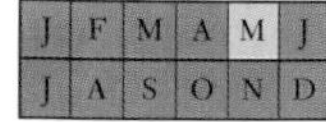

Serbian Spruce

Picea omorika

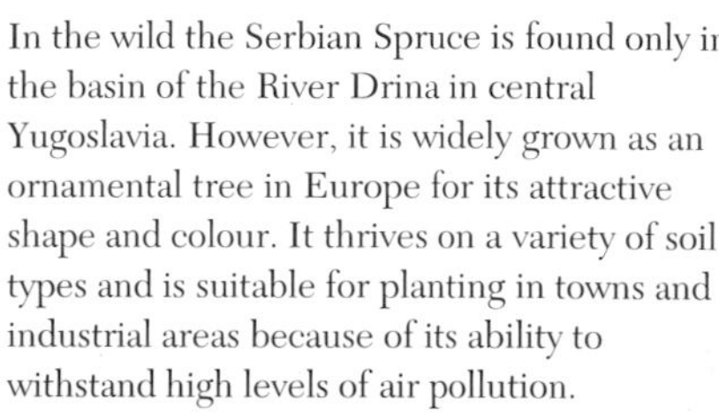

In the wild the Serbian Spruce is found only in the basin of the River Drina in central Yugoslavia. However, it is widely grown as an ornamental tree in Europe for its attractive shape and colour. It thrives on a variety of soil types and is suitable for planting in towns and industrial areas because of its ability to withstand high levels of air pollution.

ID FACT FILE

CROWN:
Narrow spire; branched almost from ground level

BARK:
Red-brown, flaking

LEAVES:
Flattened needles 8–18 mm, blunt, blue-green with 2 broad, whitish bands beneath. Upper needles point forwards, lower spread to form a parting beneath shoot. Persistent, peg-like bases

CONES:
3–6 cm, cylindrical but tapering, crimson at first maturing to reddish-brown, pendulous. Scales rounded at tips

PINE FAMILY, PINACEAE

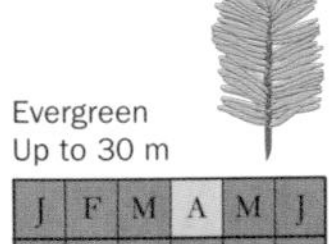

Evergreen
Up to 30 m

J	F	M	A	M	J
J	A	S	O	N	D

White Spruce

Picea glauca

ID FACT FILE

Crown:
Narrowly conical but rounded in older trees

Bark:
Cracking into rounded plates

Leaves:
Needles about 12 mm, 4-sided, blunt, stiff, strong bluish-green and smelling unpleasant when crushed; spreading to form a parting beneath shoot; persistent, peg-like bases

Cones:
2.5–6 cm, cylindrical or cigar-shaped, orange-brown and pendulous when mature. Scales rounded

White Spruce is best known for its attractive leaves which can be pale bluish-green but in some forms are an intense bluish colour. When crushed the foliage smells unpleasant to some people. White Spruce is planted as both an ornamental and a timber tree in N Europe. It is native to northern parts of the USA and Canada.

Evergreen
Up to 30 m

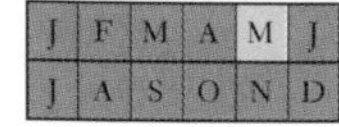

Eastern Hemlock-spruce

Tsuga canadensis

ID FACT FILE

Crown:
Cylindrical

Bark:
Grey, ageing purple-brown, flaking

Leaves:
Flattened needles of different lengths from 8 to 18 mm, blunt, hard, dark green with 2 narrow, white bands beneath. Needles on upper side are twisted to show pale bands, others spread to sides. Persistent, cushion-like bases

Cones:
1.5–2 cm, pendulous, red-brown. Scales few

Lookalikes:
Spruces (pp.15–21)

Eastern and Western Hemlock-spruces originate from the eastern and western parts of N America respectively. They are similar in general appearance but the eastern species forms a much smaller and broader tree and the needles have narrower white bands on the underside. The crushed foliage supposedly smells like the unrelated Hemlock, a poisonous herb of the Carrot family.

Evergreen
Up to 70 m

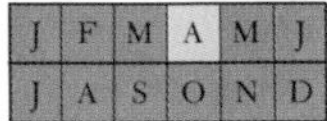

Western Hemlock-spruce

Tsuga heterophylla

ID FACT FILE

Crown:
Conical, almost branched from ground level

Bark:
Grey, ageing purple-brown, flaking

Leaves:
Flattened needles of different lengths, blunt, 6–20 mm, hard, dark green with 2 broad white bands beneath; spreading to sides of shoot; persistent, cushion-like bases

Cones:
2–2.5 cm, pendulous, red-brown. Scales few

Lookalikes:
Spruces (pp.15–21)

Hemlock-spruces are similar to true spruces but lack the distinctive small pegs which are left behind on the shoots when Spruce needles fall. Instead, Hemlock-spruce needles have cushion-like bases which persist on the shoots. Western Hemlock-spruce is the larger of the two species commonly planted in Europe and forms a graceful, narrow-crowned tree with a distinctive, drooping leading shoot.

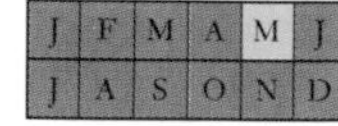

Evergreen
Up to 55 m

J	F	M	A	M	J
J	A	S	O	N	D

Douglas Fir

Pseudotsuga menziesii

ID FACT FILE

Crown:
Conical. Branches in irregular whorls

Bark:
Grey to purple-brown, corky and ridged

Leaves:
Narrow needles 20–35 mm, pointed but soft, dark green with 2 white bands beneath, aromatic when crushed; spreading to sides of shoot. Leaf-scars raised, elliptical

Cones:
5–10 cm, brown, pendulous. A long, 3-toothed bract projects beneath each scale

Lookalikes:
Spruces (pp.15-21)

In its native western N America some specimens of Douglas Fir are among the tallest trees in the world, exceeding 100 m in height. Trees grown in Europe flourish in damp regions but rarely reach anywhere near this size. Widely planted, Douglas Fir is easily recognised by the cones which have long, three-toothed bracts beneath the cone-scales. It sometimes exceeds its normal maximum height of 55 m.

Evergreen
Up to 30 m

J	F	M	A	M	J
J	A	S	O	N	D

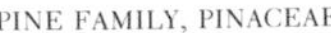

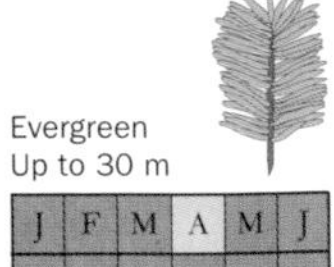

Shore Pine

Pinus contorta

ID FACT FILE

Crown:
Bushy when young, narrow in old trees. Branches short and twisted

Bark:
Corky, cracking into square plates

Leaves:
Very slender, paired needles 30–70 mm, twisted, pointed, yellow-green

Cones:
2–6 cm, in clusters of 2–4, ripe in the second year. Scales tipped with a slender spike

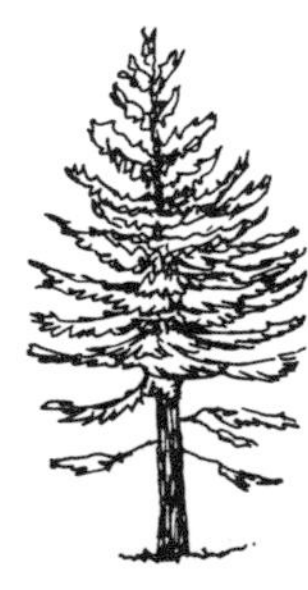

Named for its twisted branches which, together with the needles, give the tree a contorted appearance. Initially bushy, the crown becomes taller and narrow with age. The straight trunk is often short. Shore Pine is native to the west coast of N America. Because it grows well on poor and wet soils it has been widely planted in NW and central Europe in areas where other pines struggle to survive.

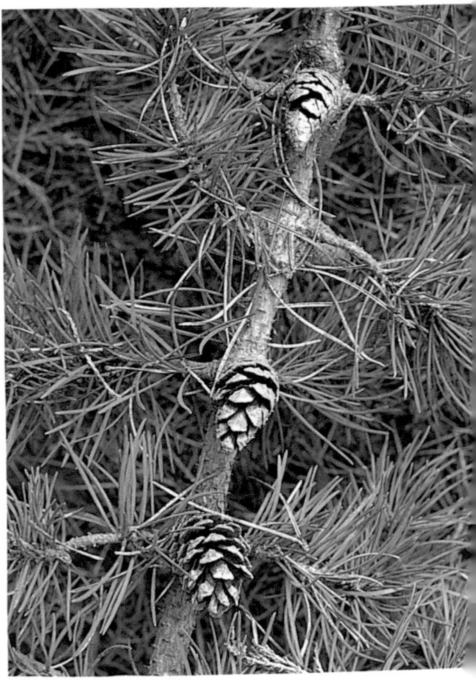

Evergreen
Up to 35 m

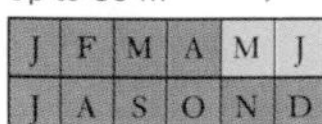

Scots Pine

Pinus sylvestris

ID FACT FILE

Crown:
Small, flat-topped, usually irregular

Bark:
Reddish–brown, paler and papery towards top of trunk

Leaves:
Paired needles 25–80 mm, twisted, finely toothed, grey or blue-green with a grey sheath at base of each pair

Cones:
2–8 cm, in clusters of 1–3, ripening to dull grey in second year. Scales have a flat or pyramidal apex and a short spine

Scots Pine is easily recognised by its distinctive long, bare, reddish-brown trunk and small, lop-sided crown. It is widespread in Europe and is the only species of pine native to Britain. Extensive natural pine forests are now restricted to Scotland but small woods and individual trees occur in many areas and Scots Pine is widely planted for timber.

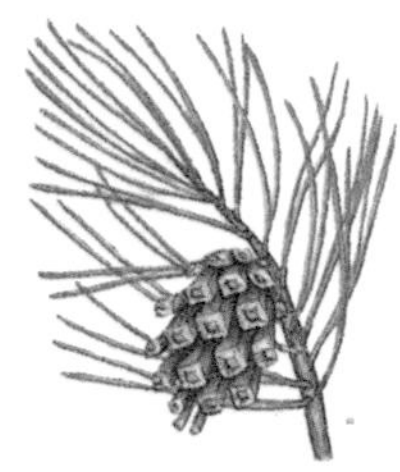

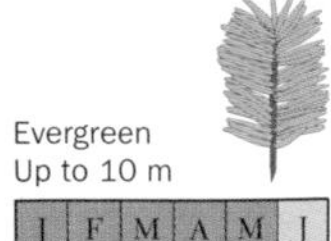

Evergreen
Up to 10 m

J	F	M	A	M	J
J	A	S	O	N	D

Dwarf Mountain Pine

Pinus mugo

ID FACT FILE

Crown:
Shrubby, with numerous spreading, twisted branches

Bark:
Brown

Leaves:
Paired needles 30–80 mm, stiff, curved, bright green

Cones:
2–5 cm, in clusters of 1–3, shiny, brown, ripe in second year. Apex of scales flat except for raised centre bearing small spine

An upland species native to the high mountains of central Europe and the Balkan Peninsula. Dwarf Mountain Pine grows in severe conditions and, although it can form a small tree, it is more usually seen as a stunted, shrubby plant up to about 3 m, rarely reaching its maximum height. It is planted as protection from winds and avalanches in mountain regions, and as a sand-binder in N Europe.

Evergreen
Up to 40 m

J	F	M	A	M	J
J	A	S	O	N	D

Corsican Pine

Pinus nigra subsp. *laricio*

Corsican Pine and Austrian Pine are both subspecies of *Pinus nigra* and are very similar to each other. Corsican Pine has fewer, shorter branches, and paler, softer foliage with grey-green, flexible needles. Unlike Austrian Pine it is a valuable timber tree. In the wild it is confined to Corsica, S Italy and Sicily but it is widely planted elsewhere in Europe.

ID FACT FILE

Crown:
Pyramidal. Foliage sparse

Bark:
Grey-brown or black, very rough

Leaves:
Paired needles arranged in whorls, 100–150 mm, soft, flexible, often twisted, grey-green

Cones:
5–8 cm, paired, ripening from pink to shiny pale brown in second year. Scales ridged and spine-tipped

Evergreen
Up to 50 m

J	F	M	A	M	J
J	A	S	O	N	D

Austrian Pine

Pinus nigra subsp. *nigra*

A widespread tree in central Europe and on the coasts of S Europe, Austrian Pine is the commonest subspecies of *Pinus nigra*. It has very dense, dark and rough foliage and very rough bark. The wood is also coarse and knotty so Austrian Pine is seldom planted for timber, but is mainly used to provide shelter.

ID FACT FILE

Crown:
Pyramidal, becoming flat-topped

Bark:
Grey-brown or black, very rough

Leaves:
Paired needles arranged in whorls, 100–150 mm, stiff, toothed, thicker at tips, very dark green

Cones:
5–8 cm, paired, ripening from pink to shiny pale brown in second year. Scales ridged and spine-tipped

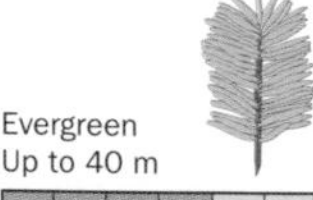

Maritime Pine

Pinus pinaster

ID FACT FILE

Crown:
Open, spreading

Bark:
Red-brown, fissured

Leaves:
Long, paired needles 100–250 mm, stiff, spiny, grey-green

Cones:
8–22 cm, ripening pale, shiny brown in second year. Apex of scales rhomboidal, ridged, with a short point

The stiff, spiny needles of Maritime Pine are longer than those of any other species of pine that has paired needles. Resin is sometimes collected in the same way as rubber, by cutting grooves in the long, bare trunk. Occurring naturally around the coastal regions of the Mediterranean, Maritime Pine is also planted on light sandy or poor soils elsewhere.

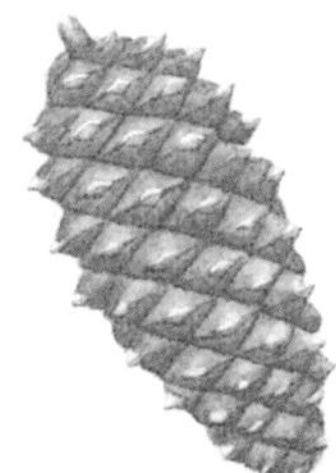

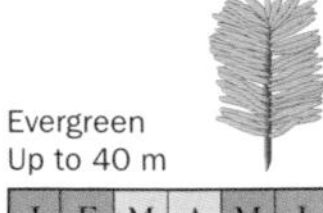

Evergreen
Up to 40 m

J	F	M	A	M	J
J	A	S	O	N	D

Monterey Pine

Pinus radiata

ID FACT FILE

CROWN:
Tall, domed

BARK:
Dark brown, thick with deep ridges

LEAVES:
Needles in threes, 100–150 cm, slender, straight, pointed and minutely toothed, bright green

CONES:
7–14 cm, in clusters of 3–5, asymmetric at base, shiny brown and recurved against the stalk when ripe. Scales have a broad apex

Probably the most common of the 3-needled pines grown in Europe. The cones will only open to release their seeds when exposed to very high temperatures. This is an adaptation to the frequent bush fires which occur in the tree's native California, allowing the seeds to germinate in newly cleared areas after the fires have passed.

Evergreen
Up to 75 m

J	F	M	A	M	J
J	A	S	O	N	D

Western Yellow Pine

Pinus ponderosa

ID FACT FILE

CROWN:
Conical, with branches drooping

BARK:
Yellowish- or reddish-brown, thick, scaly

LEAVES:
Needles in threes, 100–250 mm, stout, stiff, curved, yellowish-green, aromatic

CONES:
8–15 cm, sometimes in clusters, reddish-brown and spreading away from shoot or slightly recurved when ripe. Scales have a ribbed apex; the central boss has an erect spine

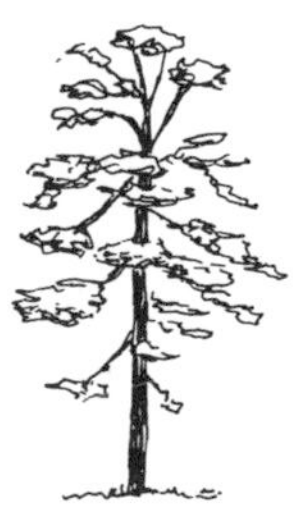

Probably the tallest pine planted in Europe, this species comes from western N America where it is common and widespread. It is aptly named for its deep yellowish-green needles and is usually grown as an ornamental tree. The cones are reddish-brown and often leave the lowest few cone-scales on the twig when they are shed.

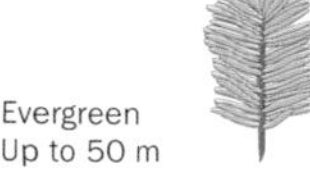

Evergreen
Up to 50 m

Weymouth Pine

Pinus strobus

ID FACT FILE

Crown:
Broadly pyramidal

Bark:
Grey-green ageing to brown, cracked

Leaves:
Needles in fives, dense, 50–140 mm, flexible, bluish-green. Those of young shoots have tuft of reddish down at base

Cones:
8–20 cm, cylindrical or curved at tip, sticky, pendulous. Ripe in second year

A native of N America, this is one of the 5-needled pines and is easily distinguished from similar species by the tuft of hairs at the base of each bundle of needles. Once widely grown in Europe for timber and occasionally as an ornamental, it is vulnerable to blister rust, a fungal disease which killed many trees, so it is less common nowadays.

Evergreen
Up to 30 m

J	F	M	A	M	J
J	A	S	O	N	D

Macedonian Pine

Pinus peuce

ID FACT FILE

Crown:
Narrowly conical

Bark:
Grey, thin and scaly

Leaves:
Needles in fives, dense and forward-pointing, 70–120 mm, slender, stiff, sharp, green

Cones:
8–15 cm, sometimes in clusters, curved, ripening brown and sticky with resin. Scales broadly wedge-shaped

Macedonian Pine is somewhat similar in appearance to the introduced Bhutan Pine but has smaller and less spreading needles, and smaller cones. In the wild this rare tree is restricted to the mountains of the Balkan Peninsula but it is planted for timber elsewhere, especially in exposed upland regions.

Evergreen
Up to 50 m

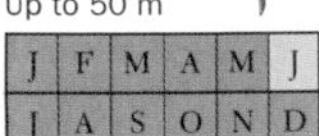

Bhutan Pine

Pinus wallichiana

ID FACT FILE

Crown:
Spreading. Branches drooping

Bark:
Grey-brown, smooth to finely cracked

Leaves:
Needles in fives, drooping on older shoots, 80–200 mm, flexible but sharp, grey-green

Cones:
15–25 cm, in clusters of 1–3, cylindrical, pendulous, brown and sticky with resin in second year. Scales vertically grooved

An elegant tree, the branches, needles and cones all drooping. The crown is quite narrow and compact in young trees but becomes broader, more open and spreading as the tree ages. Native to high, cool regions of the Himalayas, Bhutan Pine withstands pollution and is grown both for timber and as an ornamental tree.

Deciduous
Up to 35 m

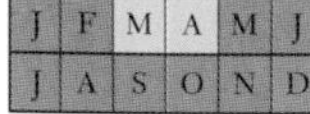

European Larch

Larix decidua

ID FACT FILE

Crown: Conical, becoming broader. Shoots pendulous

Bark: Grey to brownish, cracked

Leaves: Flattened needles 12–30 mm, soft, pale green, scattered on long shoots, in dense rosettes on spur-like short shoots

Cones: 2–3 cm, ovoid. Scales softly hairy and close-pressed

Larches are deciduous conifers with shoots of two kinds; long shoots with scattered needles and short spur-like shoots with rosettes of 30–40 needles. The needles turn red and then yellow in autumn before falling. European Larch is a short-lived, fast-growing tree native to mountains of central and E Europe but widely planted for timber and naturalised in many places.

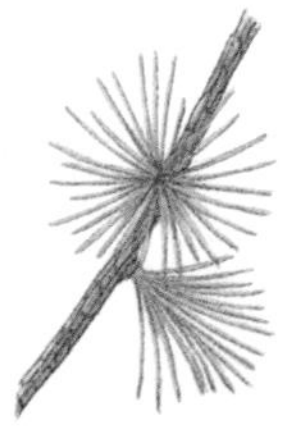

Deciduous
Up to 40 m

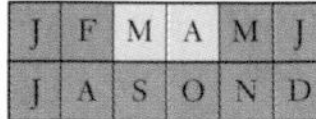

Japanese Larch

Larix kaempferi

ID FACT FILE

Crown:
Broadly conical

Bark:
Reddish-brown

Leaves:
Flattened needles 12–30 mm, soft, blue- or grey-green with 2 white bands beneath; scattered on long shoots, in dense rosettes on spur-like short shoots

Cones:
1.5–3.5 cm, ovoid. Scales softly hairy, curved outwards along upper edge

This Japanese species has foliage of a more bluish or grey hue than European Larch and lacks pendulous shoots. The upper edges of the cone-scales curve outwards slightly, giving the cones a rose-like appearance. Japanese Larch is a vigorous grower and is often used in commercial plantations. It hybridises with European Larch, giving offspring intermediate between the parents.

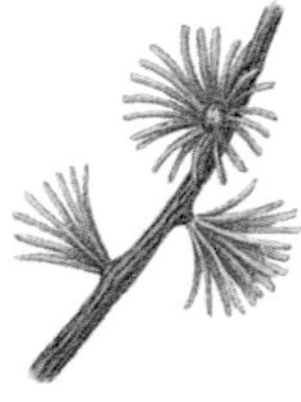

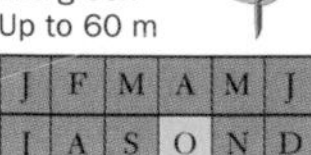

Evergreen
Up to 60 m

J	F	M	A	M	J
J	A	S	O	N	D

Deodar

Cedrus deodara

ID FACT FILE

Crown: Triangular, branches curved down

Bark: Almost black

Leaves: Needles 3-sided, 20–50 mm, pale green, those of short shoots in rosettes of 15–20

Cones: 8–12 cm, erect, barrel-shaped, tip rounded. Ripe in second year

Like larches, cedars (including the Deodar) have long and short shoots, the short ones with rosettes of needles. Deodar has a triangular outline, down-swept branches and a distinctly drooping leading shoot. Both male and female cones are large, the barrel-shaped females being solid and breaking up on the tree when ripe to leave only the persistent central spike. An ornamental species native to the W Himalayas.

Evergreen
Up to 40 m

J	F	M	A	M	J
J	A	S	O	N	D

Atlantic Cedar

Cedrus atlantica

ID FACT FILE

CROWN:
Triangular. Branches curved upwards

BARK:
Dark grey, initially smooth, becoming rougher

LEAVES:
Needles 3-sided, 10–30 mm, green or blue-green, those of short shoots in rosettes of 10–45

CONES:
5–8 cm, erect, barrel-shaped, tip flat or dimpled. Ripe in second year

Native to the Atlas Mountains of N Africa but grown for ornament in Europe and as a timber tree in parts of the south. A pollution-tolerant form with blue-green leaves is most popular for planting in town parks. Atlantic Cedar closely resembles the Deodar but has branches angled upwards and a stiff, erect leading shoot. The female cones have a flat or dimpled, not rounded, top.

Evergreen
Up to 40 m

J	F	M	A	M	J
J	A	S	O	N	D

Cedar-of-Lebanon

Cedrus libani

ID FACT FILE

Crown:
Conical when young, becoming broad and spreading

Bark:
Grey-black, fissured

Leaves:
Needles 3-sided, 15–35 mm, dark green. Those of short shoots in rosettes of 10–15

Cones:
7–12 cm, erect, barrel-shaped, tip rounded. Ripe in second year

This is the most familiar and easily recognised of the Cedars. Slow-growing and long-lived, it only develops the characteristic flat-topped shape and level, table-like masses of foliage in old age, young trees being conical in outline. Although it produces valuable timber, it is usually seen as a magnificent specimen tree in parks and large gardens. Native to the E Mediterranean.

Deciduous
Up to 50 m

J	F	M	A	M	J
J	A	S	O	N	D

Swamp Cypress

Taxodium distichum

ID FACT FILE

CROWN:
Conical to triangular, sometimes domed

BARK:
Reddish, peeling in strings

LEAVES:
Flattened needles 8–20 mm, pale green. Spirally arranged on terminal shoots, in 2 rows on side-shoots

CONES:
1.2–3 cm, globular, purple when ripe. Scales diamond-shaped, blunt, with short, hooked spine

LOOKALIKE:
Dawn Redwood (p.42)

Swamp Cypress is also known as Bald Cypress in its native southern USA because of its deciduous nature. The tree produces yellow and red colours in autumn before shedding both its needles and the smaller side shoots. When grown in swampy ground numerous stump-like breathing roots or pneumatophores protrude up to 1m above the ground around the trunk. They do not develop when the tree grows in dry soil.

Deciduous
Up to 40 m

Dawn Redwood

Metasequoia glyptostroboides

ID FACT FILE

CROWN:
Conical

BARK:
Orange to red-brown, peeling vertically

LEAVES:
Paired shoots with flattened needles 25 mm long, pale green becoming darker

CONES:
Globular cones 2.5 cm in diameter ripen brown. Cone-scales lack spines

LOOKALIKE:
Swamp Cypress (p.41)

Once widespread, this species was known only from fossils until 1941, when a living tree was discovered in China. It survives in the wild only in remote south-western parts of that country but is grown as an ornamental tree in many parts of the world. Unlike other redwoods it is deciduous, shedding both needles and short shoots in the same way as Swamp Cypress.

Evergreen
Up to 110 m

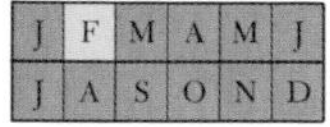

J	F	M	A	M	J
J	A	S	O	N	D

Coast Redwood

Sequoia sempervirens

ID FACT FILE

Crown: Columnar, narrow

Bark: Flaking to reveal thick, reddish, fibrous inner bark

Leaves: Scales 6 mm on terminal and cone-bearing shoots. Needles 6–20 mm with 2 white bands beneath and arranged in 2 rows on side-shoots

Cones: 1.8–2.5 cm, ovoid, ripe in second year. Scales dimpled

The tallest living tree in the world is a Coast Redwood in the Humbolt Redwoods State Park in California which is a little over 110 m high. Coast Redwoods are found in the wild only in the coastal hills of California and Oregon where the slopes are permanently shrouded in mist. The trees have an unusually soft, thick and fibrous inner bark which is exposed when the hard outer bark flakes away.

Evergreen
Up to 90 m

J	F	M	A	M	J
J	A	S	O	N	D

Wellingtonia

Sequoiadendron giganteum

ID FACT FILE

CROWN:
Conical, trunk very thick

BARK:
Reddish-brown, thick, spongy

LEAVES:
Scale-like, 4–10 mm, spiralled. All but tips pressed against shoot

CONES:
5–8 cm, ovoid with rounded tips. Scales dimpled, wrinkled, sometimes with a small spine

Like the related Coast Redwood, Wellingtonia or Giant Redwood is restricted to California, on the wet, western slopes of the Sierra Nevada mountains. Although generally not as tall as Coast Redwoods, Wellingtonias tend to be more massive and a specimen measured in 1968 was acknowledged as the world's bulkiest living thing.

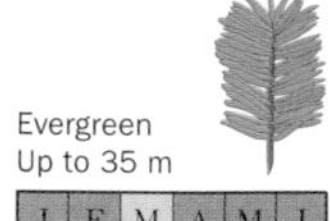

Evergreen
Up to 35 m

J	F	M	A	M	J
J	A	S	O	N	D

Japanese Red Cedar

Cryptomeria japonica

ID FACT FILE

Crown:
Conical. Branches irregularly whorled

Bark:
Pale red, thick, peeling in strips

Leaves:
Needles 6–15 mm, somewhat 4-sided, curved inwards, spirally arranged on shoot, bright green

Cones:
1.2–3 cm, globular. Scales have 5 hooked spines in centre

Japanese Red Cedar is native to both China and Japan, where it sometimes forms almost pure forests. These trees can reach considerable size and a great age, with some Japanese specimens thought to be well over 1000 years old. The tree was unknown to western science until 1701 and not introduced to Europe until 1842. It is now widely planted in parts of Europe, where most trees are still well under 100 years old.

Evergreen
Up to 25 m

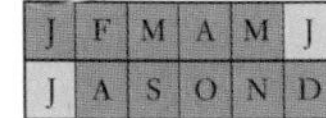

Monkey Puzzle

Araucaria araucana

ID FACT FILE

CROWN:
Broadly triangular

BARK:
Grey, ridged and wrinkled with circular scars

LEAVES:
Scale-like, 30–40 mm, triangular, rigid, dark green: in overlapping whorls around shoot

CONES:
Males 10 cm, brown, in clusters; females 10–17 cm, solitary, globular, ripening in second year. Scales leaf-like with golden tips

A curious and distinctive tree which is impossible to mistake for any other. On its introduction to Britain the stiff branches and rigid, pointed leaves were said to be sufficient to puzzle even a monkey wishing to climb it. Native to Chile and Argentina where it forms open forests, Monkey Puzzle is often planted as an unusual ornamental. Trees are either male or female.

Evergreen
Up to 65 m

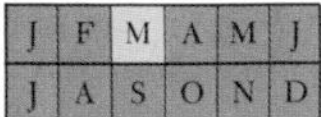

Western Red Cedar

Thuja plicata

ID FACT FILE

CROWN:
Conical to pyramidal. Apical shoot erect

BARK:
Reddish, shredding

LEAVES: In flattened sprays. Resin-scented. Alternating pairs of scales 2–3 mm, glossy green with faint white markings beneath

CONES:
1.2 cm, ovoid, ripening brown. Scales 10–12, leafy, overlapping, with a hook at tip of inner face

LOOKALIKES:
Cypresses (pp.48–53)

Not related to Japanese Red Cedar, this species originates from western N America where its strong, lightweight timber was used for making canoes and totem poles. Widely planted in much of Europe. It is related to and most easily confused with the Cypresses, especially Lawson Cypress from which it can be distinguished by its erect leading shoot.

Evergreen
Up to 36 m

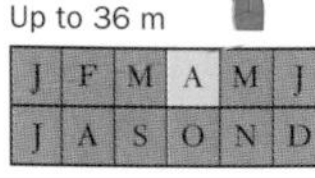

Hinoki Cypress

Chamaecyparis obtusa

ID FACT FILE

Crown:
Broadly conical

Bark:
Reddish, shredding

Leaves:
In flattened sprays. Sweetly resin-scented. Scales about 2 mm, green, those on lower side of shoot have white markings

Cones:
8 mm, globular, ripening from bluish-green to brown. Scales 8; central depression with a ridge

A slow-growing species which can form large trees in its native Japan. It is commonly planted as an ornamental tree in Europe, particularly in areas with wet summers such as Britain. It can be distinguished from the similar and more common Lawson Cypress by the blunt scale-leaves with X- or Y-shaped markings which smell resinous when crushed.

Evergreen
Up to 45 m

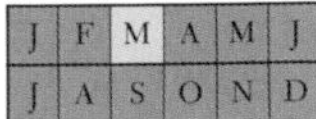

Lawson Cypress

Chamaecyparis lawsoniana

ID FACT FILE

Crown:
Spire-like. Apical shoot nodding

Bark:
Grey-brown, cracked in plates

Leaves:
In flattened, pendulous sprays. Parsley scented. Paired scales about 2 mm, usually dark green on upper side of shoot, marked with white on lower side

Cones:
8 mm, globular. Scales 8; central depression with a ridge

This is probably the most commonly planted ornamental park tree and occurs in many cultivated forms which differ mainly in the colours of their leaves. The foliage of all forms smells of parsley when crushed. Native to western N America where it can form large trees over 60 m high. Many of the trees in Europe have still to achieve their maximum growth.

Evergreen
Up to 24 m

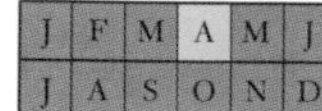

Sawara Cypress

Chamaecyparis pisifera

ID FACT FILE

Crown:
Usually conical to columnar

Bark:
Red-brown, peeling in strips

Leaves:
In flattened, pendulous sprays. Sharply resin-scented. Paired scales about 2 mm, marked with white on lower side, tips incurved

Cones:
8 mm, globular. Scales 8, wrinkled

Another Japanese species which is easily mistaken for Lawson Cypress. Sawara Cypress has paler, more delicate foliage which is acridly resinous when crushed and the crown is more open, with level branches. As with Lawson Cypress, many cultivated forms are grown, especially a golden-leaved form.

Evergreen
Up to 30 m

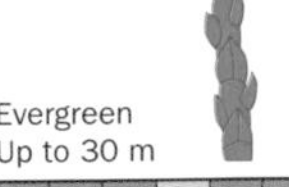

Nootka Cypress

Chamaecyparis nootkatensis

ID FACT FILE

CROWN:
Conical. Branches upturned, shoots drooping

BARK:
Orange- to grey-brown

LEAVES:
In flattened, pendulous sprays. Unpleasant-smelling. Paired scales 2–3 mm, margins pale, tips spreading

CONES:
10 mm, globular, ripening from blue to brown. Scales 8, each with a curved central spine

This very hardy species is native to northern N America up into the Arctic Circle. The crushed foliage gives off an unpleasant smell variously described as oily or like that of turpentine. Despite this, Nootka Cypress is often planted as an ornamental in Europe, especially a golden-leaved form and one in which the pendulous side-shoots fall in curtains.

J	F	M	A	M	J
J	A	S	O	N	D

Leyland Cypress

× Cupressocyparis leylandii

ID FACT FILE

Crown:
Narrowly columnar. Leading shoot leans but does not droop

Bark:
Reddish

Leaves:
Often in flattened sprays. Paired scales 0.5–2 mm, pointed, dark green or greyish above, yellowish beneath

Cones:
2–3 cm, globular, ripening from green to brown. Scales with blunt spike in centre, few

Leyland Cypress is seen everywhere nowadays and it is probably the most frequently planted garden conifer. Its dense foliage and extremely fast growth rate make it ideal for hedges and screens. An intergeneric hybrid between the Monterey Cypress (genus *Cupressus*) and Nootka Cypress (genus *Chamaecyparis*), it arose in cultivation and is unknown in the wild.

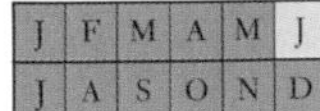

Evergreen
Up to 35 m

J	F	M	A	M	J
J	A	S	O	N	D

Monterey Cypress

Cupressus macrocarpa

ID FACT FILE

CROWN: Narrow, becoming broader and spreading

BARK: Yellowish-brown, ridged

LEAVES: Overlapping paired scales 1–2 mm, closely pressed against shoot, yellowish-green

CONES: 2–3 cm, globose, ripening brown in second year. Scales with pointed central boss, few

Unlike the genus *Chamaecyparis*, members of the genus *Cupressus* have shoots radiating in all directions, not forming flattened sprays. Monterey Cypress originates from Monterey County in California but is now rare in the wild. It was formerly much planted for screens and shelter but is less common in cultivation too, having been replaced by Leyland Cypress.

Evergreen
Up to 6 m

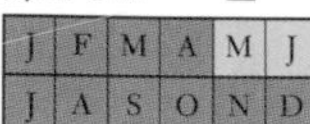

J	F	M	A	M	J
J	A	S	O	N	D

Juniper

Juniperus communis

Junipers form small trees or shrubs on lime-rich soils in most parts of Europe. They are typical of downland in the north but are confined to mountainous regions in the south. Male and female cones are borne on separate trees. Initially the female cones resemble those of cypresses but as they ripen the scales become fleshy and coalesce, forming a berry-like structure instead of a woody cone.

ID FACT FILE

CROWN:
Spreading, bushy

BARK:
Reddish, shredding

LEAVES:
Prickly, flattened needles in whorls of 3; 8–30 mm, stiff, bluish-green, upper side with broad white band

CONES:
Fleshy and berry-like, 6–9 mm, globular, ripening dull blue-black in second or third year

Evergreen
Up to 30 m

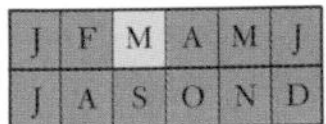

Pencil Cedar

Juniperus virginiana

ID FACT FILE

Crown:
Narrowly pyramidal

Bark:
Grey to red-brown, peeling in strips

Leaves:
Paired needles 5–6 mm, with 2 white bands beneath. Paired scales 0.5–1.5 mm, pointed, pressed to shoot. Smells unpleasant when crushed

Cones:
4–6 mm, ovoid, ripening from blue-green to brownish-violet in second year

Like the related Phoenician Juniper, Pencil Cedar bears different juvenile and adult foliage on the same tree but the needles of juvenile growth are sometimes absent in old trees. Native to eastern and central N America, Pencil Cedar is grown as an ornamental tree in Europe and for timber in central and southern parts. It is the tallest species of juniper grown in Europe.

Evergreen
Up to 25 m

J	F	M	A	M	J
J	A	S	O	N	D

Yew

Taxus baccata

ID FACT FILE

Crown:
Rounded

Bark:
Reddish, flaking

Leaves:
Flattened needles 10–30 mm, pointed, dull green above, yellowish beneath; spreading in 2 rows along shoot

Flowers:
Males yellowish, females greenish, on separate trees

Fruits:
Fleshy red cup up to 1 cm surrounding single seed 6–7 mm long

Yew trees are slow-growing and long-lived; some specimens are thought to be 1500 years old. Yew occurs throughout Europe, mainly in woods on limestone soils. The timber was valued in former times, especially for making bows. Yews are highly poisonous and were often planted in churchyards and other walled enclosures, probably to protect farm animals which readily eat the foliage, despite its fatal effect.

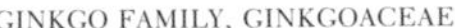

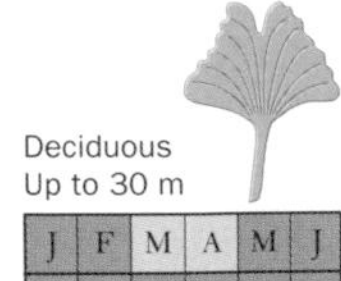

Deciduous
Up to 30 m

J	F	M	A	M	J
J	A	S	O	N	D

Maidenhair Tree

Ginkgo biloba

ID FACT FILE

Crown:
Conical but irregular

Bark:
Greyish

Leaves:
Scattered on long shoots, clustered on short shoots; 12 × 10 cm, fan-shaped with a deep apical notch, leathery

Flowers:
Males in catkins, females solitary or paired, on separate trees

Fruits:
2.5–3 cm, oval, fleshy, yellow

Originally native to China, the Maidenhair Tree is now probably extinct in the wild but is widely grown as an ornamental and park tree in many parts of the world. The fruit, which contains a large, stony seed, begins to smell very unpleasant as it ripens from green to yellow. They are eaten in China but are rarely produced in the cooler parts of Europe.
Up to 30 m.

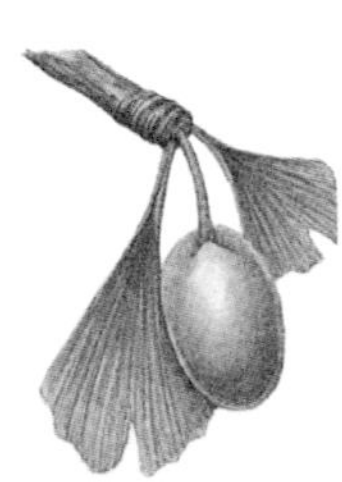

Deciduous
Up to 7 m

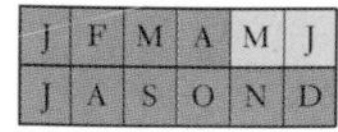

Bay Willow

Salix pentandra

ID FACT FILE

Crown:
Bushy

Twigs:
Shiny reddish-brown

Leaves:
Alternate, 5–12 cm, less than 3 times as long as wide, elliptical, shiny above

Flowers:
Catkins appear with leaves

Bay Willow is widespread in N and central Europe but is native only to some parts. Male trees have more showy catkins than female trees and are more often planted. In areas where the species is merely introduced, most or all of the trees may be male. The leaves supposedly have a similar scent to those of the Sweet Bay though in fact they smell faintly of balsam.

Deciduous
Up to 10 m

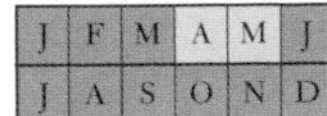

Almond Willow

Salix triandra

ID FACT FILE

CROWN:
Bushy

LEAVES:
Alternate, 4–11 cm, more than 3 times as long as wide, long-pointed, toothed, dull. Ear-shaped stipules at base

FLOWERS:
Catkins erect, appearing just before leaves. Males fragrant

Usually found growing on wetter soils, this willow is one of the main sources for basket-makers' materials. It is very variable in leaf shape and colour, catkin size and even the shape of the tree. Many of these different types occur naturally in the wild but some are the descendants of cultivated varieties formerly grown for the basket industry.

Deciduous
Up to 25 m

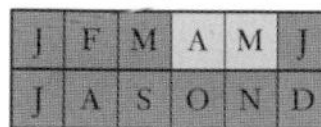

Crack Willow

Salix fragilis

ID FACT FILE

Crown:
Rounded. Trunk short and thick

Twigs:
Olive-brown, breaking easily

Leaves:
Alternate, 9–15 cm, long-pointed, coarsely toothed, shiny above

Flowers:
Catkins 4–6 cm, appearing with leaves

Crack Willow is named for the brittle quality of its twigs which readily break away at the point where they grow out from the branch. Crack Willow prefers deep soils and is almost always found in wet areas on agricultural land. Broken twigs washed down streams and rivers can root in the banks and the tree spreads easily along water-courses in this way.

Deciduous
Up to 25 m

J	F	M	A	M	J
J	A	S	O	N	D

White Willow

Salix alba

ID FACT FILE

Crown:
Narrow, branches angled upwards

Twigs:
Olive-green to brown

Leaves:
Alternate, 5–10 cm, more than 3 times as long as wide. Minutely toothed, silvery-hairy when young and remaining greyish beneath

Flowers:
Catkins erect, appearing with leaves

Widespread in Europe, White Willow is very noticeable in spring when the young leaves still have a full coating of silvery hairs. The true White Willow described here is var. *alba* but there are two other common varieties of *Salix alba*. Golden Willow (var. *vitellina*) has bright yellow or orange year-old twigs. Cricket-bat Willow (var. *caerulea*) has bluish foliage; only the wood of female trees is used to make cricket-bats.

Deciduous
Up to 12 m

J	F	M	A	M	J
J	A	S	O	N	D

Golden Weeping Willow

Salix × sepulcralis

ID FACT FILE

CROWN:
Domed. Branches hang almost to the ground

TWIGS:
Slender, golden-yellow

LEAVES:
Alternate, 7–12 cm, more than 3 times as long as wide, toothed

FLOWERS:
Catkins often curved, appearing with leaves

The true Weeping Willow from China is rarely grown in Europe and most of the trees seen in parks and along rivers are actually hardier hybrids. By far the commonest of these is Golden Weeping Willow which is more colourful and profoundly weeping than other hybrids. It is a cross between Weeping and Golden Willows but little else is known of its history.

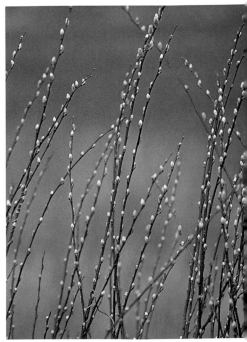

Deciduous
Up to 10 m

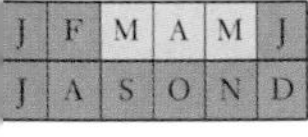

Grey Sallow

Salix cinerea

ID FACT FILE

Crown:
Broad, with branches spreading

Twigs:
Thickly grey-hairy when young

Leaves:
Alternate, 2–16 cm, less than 3 times as long as wide, grey-hairy beneath, toothed margins rolled under. Ear-shaped stipules at base

Flowers:
Catkins erect, appearing before leaves

Also called Grey Willow, this tree is named for the ash-coloured hairs which densely cover the young twigs and the undersides of the leaves. The silky-hairy catkins are also grey and, like Goat Willow, are often referred to as 'pussy willows'. A subspecies of Grey Sallow with red-brown twigs and leaves with rusty-coloured hairs beneath is separated as the Rusty Sallow.

Deciduous
Up to 10 m

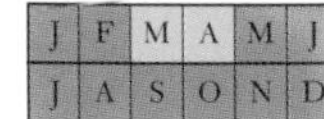

Goat Willow

Salix caprea

ID FACT FILE

Crown:
Open, spreading

Twigs:
Stout, stiff, yellow-brown

Leaves:
Alternate, 5–12 cm, broadly oval to oblong, grey-hairy above, woolly beneath, irregularly toothed. Small stipules at base

Flowers:
Catkins erect, mostly at twig tips, appearing before leaves

Common throughout Europe, Goat Willow tolerates drier habitats than other willows and is often found along hedgerows and the edges of woods. It is one of the first of the willows to flower. The female catkins especially are smooth and silky-hairy and are the 'pussy willows' picked in spring. In winter the yellow-brown twigs develop a distinctive reddish stain on the most exposed surface.

Deciduous
Up to 6 m

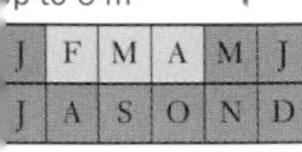

Osier

Salix viminalis

ID FACT FILE

Crown:
Narrow

Twigs:
Long, grey-hairy becoming shiny olive or brown

Leaves:
Alternate, 10–15 cm, tapering, margins often wavy or rolled under, silvery-hairy beneath

Flowers:
Catkins erect, crowded at twig tips, appearing before leaves

Osier is common almost everywhere in wet, lowland habitats but is probably introduced in many areas. It is a favourite species for basket-making and is often planted to form osier beds. Here the trees are pollarded to leave a short trunk with a rounded head of long, pliant twigs which are regularly cropped. These twigs are the 'withies' used for baskets, lobster-pots and other cane-work.

Deciduous
Up to 12 m

European Violet Willow

Salix daphnoides

ID FACT FILE

Crown:
Rounded. Branches erect to spreading

Twigs:
Violet with a waxy-blue bloom

Leaves:
Alternate, 7–12 cm, less than 3 times as long as wide, evenly toothed. Stipules usually present at base

Flowers:
Catkins erect, conspicuously black-flecked, appearing before leaves

Similar in general appearance to Purple Willow, European Violet Willow has twigs with a dense, waxy bloom when young although this gradually rubs off leaving the twigs rather shiny. They are particularly noticeable in winter. The colourful twigs and shiny leaves make this tree a popular ornamental, often planted outside its native central Europe.

Deciduous
Up to 20 m

J	F	M	A	M	J
J	A	S	O	N	D

White Poplar

Populus alba

ID FACT FILE

Crown:
Spreading

Bark:
Grey with black bars

Leaves:
Alternate, 3–9 cm, with irregular lobes, densely white-hairy beneath. Stalk cylindrical

Flowers:
Catkins appear before leaves. Males purplish, females greenish

White Poplar readily produces suckers which spread underground for a considerable distance before emerging and which often form thickets around the parent tree. The leaves are two-coloured, the hairy, white lower surface contrasting strikingly with the hairless, dark green upper surface. White Poplar is native to Europe though it is introduced in many areas. It prefers soft, wet ground.

Deciduous
Up to 30 m

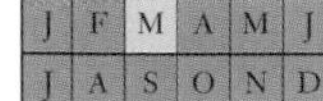

Grey Poplar

Populus × canescens

ID FACT FILE

CROWN:
Spreading

BARK:
Grey with black bars

LEAVES:
Alternate. On leading shoots 6–8 cm, coarsely toothed, grey-hairy beneath; on side-shoots smaller, broader, wavy-toothed and hairless. Stalk flattened on sides

FLOWERS:
Catkins 5–8 cm, appearing before leaves. Males purplish, females pinkish

This tree is a natural hybrid between White Poplar and Aspen. It has some of the characteristics of each parent, such as the grey trunk of White Poplar but leaves more like Aspen. It is native or introduced in much of Europe although it has a more northerly distribution than the White Poplar. Male trees are much more common than female ones.

Deciduous
Up to 20 m

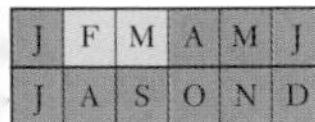

Aspen

Populus tremula

ID FACT FILE

CROWN:
Broad, sometimes conical

BARK:
Grey, smooth

LEAVES:
Alternate, 1.5–8 cm, bluntly toothed, very pale beneath. Stalk flattened on sides

FLOWERS:
Catkins appear before leaves; males purplish, females pinkish

This is the most widespread of the European poplars and is found almost throughout the region. Aspens are renowned for the near-continuous motion of their 'trembling' leaves. This is due to the lateral flattening of the leaf-stalks which allows the leaves to flutter in the faintest air currents. The movement is accentuated by the flashing of the pale lower surfaces of the leaves.

Deciduous
Up to 35 m

Black Poplar

Populus nigra

ID FACT FILE

Crown: Broad, rounded. Trunk has rough swellings

Bark: Grey, fissured

Leaves: Alternate, 5–10 cm, finely toothed. Stalk flattened on sides

Flowers: Catkins appear before leaves; males crimson, females greenish

Black Poplar forms a robust tree, the trunk often with large swellings and numerous twiggy outgrowths. Unlike those of other common European species the finely toothed leaves are smooth and only slightly paler on the lower surface than on the upper. The leaves have laterally flattened stalks and are able to flutter like those of Aspen but the movement is less pronounced.

Deciduous
Up to 35 m

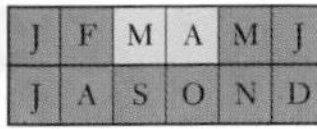

Lombardy Poplar

Populus nigra var. *italica*

ID FACT FILE

CROWN:
Tall and very narrow, branches held almost vertically

BARK:
Grey, fissured

LEAVES:
Alternate, 5–10 cm, finely toothed. Stalk flattened on sides

FLOWERS:
Catkins appear before leaves

Instantly recognisable by its tall and very narrow outline, Lombardy Poplar is usually planted in straight lines along roads and avenues. It is thought to have arisen in the Lombardy region of N Italy around the late 17th or early 18th centuries and is now seen everywhere in Europe. It must be propagated by cuttings as the trees are always male.

Deciduous
Up to 30 m

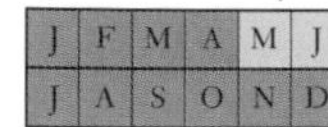

Walnut

Juglans regia

ID FACT FILE

CROWN:
Spreading. Branches twisting

BARK:
Grey, smooth, later fissured

LEAVES:
Alternate, leathery and aromatic, pinnate. Leaflets 7–9, 6–15 cm, basal smallest

FLOWERS:
Small, greenish. Males in catkins 5–15 cm, females in clusters of 2–5

FRUITS:
4–5 cm. Green, fleshy husk surrounding wrinkled stone

Native to SE Europe, the Walnut has been cultivated in many other areas since ancient times. Male and female flowers occur on the same tree, the males on new growth, the females on old wood. The familiar walnut is actually the stone enclosed within the otherwise inedible fruit. An old saying advises beating Walnut trees to increase their yield, though there is little evidence to suggest this works.

Deciduous
Up to 30 m

J	F	M	A	M	J
J	A	S	O	N	D

Caucasian Wingnut

Pterocarya fraxinifolia

ID FACT FILE

Crown: Broad. Trunk short

Bark: Grey, fissured

Leaves: Alternate, pinnate. Leaflets numerous, up to 18 cm; central ones largest, all unequal at base

Flowers: In catkins. Males 5–12 cm, females 10–15 cm but up to 50 cm in fruit

Fruits: In catkins. Greenish nuts each surrounded by broad, disc-like wing

Caucasian Wingnut belongs to the same family as the Walnut and has similarly divided leaves. Both male and female catkins are many-flowered and hang down from the branches. The females elongate greatly as the greenish winged nuts ripen and become very conspicuous. The tree is planted solely for ornament as the nuts are inedible.

Deciduous
Up to 20 m

J	F	M	A	M	J
J	A	S	O	N	D

Common Alder

Alnus glutinosa

ID FACT FILE

Crown:
Broadly conical. Young twigs sticky

Bark:
Grey

Leaves:
Alternate, 4–10 cm. Margins doubly toothed

Flowers:
Catkins appear before leaves. Males 2–6 cm, pendulous; females 1.5 cm, ovoid, stalked, in clusters

Fruits:
Woody, cone-like, 1–3 cm

Common Alders are typically found on marshy soils along streams and rivers and may be the dominant trees in wet places. The roots harbour nitrogen-fixing bacteria which enable the trees to thrive in such soils. The woody fruits superficially resemble the cones of pines and other conifers but have a completely different anatomical structure.

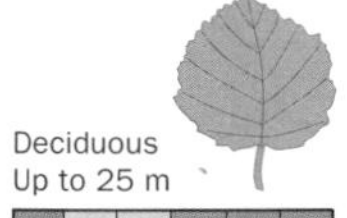

Deciduous
Up to 25 m

J	F	M	A	M	J
J	A	S	O	N	D

Grey Alder

Alnus incana

ID FACT FILE

CROWN:
Broad. Young twigs not sticky

BARK:
Grey, smooth

LEAVES:
Alternate, 4–10 cm, grey-hairy beneath, margins doubly toothed

FLOWERS:
Catkins appear before leaves. Males 2–6 cm, pendulous; females 1.5 cm, ovoid, stalkless, in clusters

FRUITS:
Woody, cone-like, 1–3 cm

Very similar to Common Alder but the young twigs and leaves are grey-hairy. It is a common tree in N Europe, extending into Arctic regions, but also occurs in mountains in the south. As with all alders, the old cones remain on the tree long after the seeds have been shed and are very noticeable on the bare branches in winter.

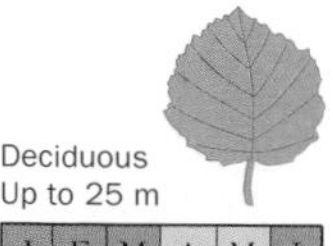

Deciduous
Up to 25 m

J	F	M	A	M	J
J	A	S	O	N	D

Downy Birch

Betula pubescens

A short-lived, cold-tolerant species widespread in Europe, especially in the north and in mountains where it forms extensive forests. Normally a small tree, in harsh or exposed areas it grows as a shrub. The male catkins are formed at the tips of twigs at the beginning of winter, ready to mature and shed pollen the following spring.

ID FACT FILE

CROWN:
Branches erect to spreading

BARK:
Brown or grey. Smooth base

LEAVES:
Alternate, up to 5.5 cm with rounded or triangular base, coarsely toothed

FLOWERS:
Male catkins 3–6 cm, pendulous at tips of twigs; females 1–4 cm in leaf axils

FRUITS:
Tiny, winged nutlets released when female catkins break up

Deciduous
Up to 30 m

J	F	M	A	M	J
J	A	S	O	N	D

Silver Birch

Betula pendula

ID FACT FILE

Crown:
Slender. Branches pendulous at tips

Bark:
Silvery

Leaves:
Alternate, up to 5 cm with base heartshaped or cut straight across, doubly toothed

Flowers:
Male catkins at tips of twigs; females in leaf axils

Fruits:
Tiny, winged nutlets

An elegant, slender tree with distinctive silvery-white bark. The bark is mostly smooth but breaks up into darker, rectangular plates at the base of the trunk. A fast-growing, short-lived species. Groves of saplings may spring up as early colonisers where other trees have fallen or been cut down before becoming shaded out by taller, slower-growing species.

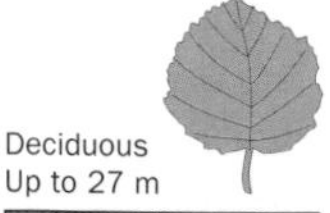

Deciduous
Up to 27 m

J	F	M	A	M	J
J	A	S	O	N	D

Paper-bark Birch

Betula papyrifera

ID FACT FILE

Crown:
Branches erect to spreading

Bark:
White, rarely brownish

Leaves:
Alternate, 4–10 cm, doubly toothed

Flowers:
Male catkins up to 10 cm; females 1–4 cm

Fruits:
Tiny, winged nutlets

Paper-bark Birch is a N American species resembling the Silver Birch of Europe. The bark is sometimes brown in young trees but is usually white and peels in broad, horizontal strips. Stretched over a light wooden frame and waterproofed, it was used by N American Indians for the construction of canoes. Often planted for ornament.

Deciduous
Up to 30 m

J	F	M	A	M	J
J	A	S	O	N	D

Hornbeam

Carpinus betulus

ID FACT FILE

Crown: Trunk and branches often twisted

Bark: Grey, fissured

Leaves: Alternate, 4–10 cm, oval, doubly toothed

Flowers: Leafy catkins: yellow males up to 5 cm; green females up to 2 cm

Fruits: Paired nuts attached to 3-lobed, leaf-like involucre

Hornbeams provide valuable hardwood timber and in the past were frequently pollarded or coppiced. When left to grow naturally they form broad, spreading trees with thick and often twisted trunks and branches. The fruiting catkins are made up of green, leaf-like structures called involucres, each of which has two nuts attached at the base.

Deciduous
Up to 12 m

J	F	M	A	M	J
J	A	S	O	N	D

Hazel

Corylus avellana

ID FACT FILE

Crown:
Shrubby, spreading

Bark:
Smooth, peeling in thin, horizontal strips

Leaves:
Alternate, up to 10 cm, very broadly oval, doubly toothed, rough and bristly to the touch

Flowers:
Appearing before leaves; males in catkins, females very small, in clusters

Fruits:
Nut enveloped in green, leafy cup

A very common hedgerow and woodland species throughout Europe. It often grows as a shrub and is frequently coppiced. Hazels are among the first trees to flower in spring, the bright yellow male catkins hanging from the bare branches as early as January. The hard-shelled nuts are each surrounded by a ragged-tipped, leafy cup or involucre and contain an edible kernel.

Deciduous
Up to 30 m

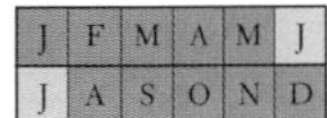

Sweet Chestnut

Castanea sativa

ID FACT FILE

CROWN:
Tall, uneven

BARK:
Greyish, spirally grooved

LEAVES:
Alternate, 10–25 cm, oblong, pointed, sharp-toothed

FLOWERS:
Erect catkins with yellow male flowers in upper part, green females below

FRUITS:
Shiny, red-brown nuts enclosed in spiny husk

Although native to S Europe, Sweet Chestnut has been widely planted elsewhere for its edible nuts. Between one and three nuts are enclosed in a rather softly but densely spiny husk which splits while still on the tree to release them. The Sweet Chestnut should not be confused with the unrelated horse-chestnuts which have fewer, tougher spines and nuts which are inedible.

Deciduous
Up to 40 m

J	F	M	A	M	J
J	A	S	O	N	D

Beech

Fagus sylvatica

ID FACT FILE

Crown:
Broadly domed

Bark:
Smooth, grey

Leaves:
Alternate, oval to elliptical, edges wavy

Flowers:
Males in drooping, long-stalked heads; females paired

Fruits:
Spiny, 4-lobed husk containing 2 small, triangular nuts

Beech woods are characteristic of limestone regions. The leaves are very slow to rot and improve the soil, and in pure beech woods a deep layer of dead leaves builds up on the ground. This prevents other plants from growing well, so beech woods have few woodland flowers. Beech nuts, or mast, are much-loved by pigs which were often turned into the woods to forage in autumn.

Deciduous
Up to 23 m

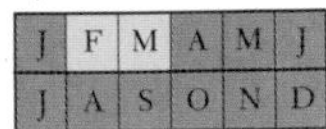

Roble Beech

Nothofagus obliqua

ID FACT FILE

Crown:
Tall, open. Branches arching

Bark:
Initially smooth, becoming rough and cracked; grey

Leaves:
Alternate, oval to elliptical with unequal base. Edges irregularly toothed

Flowers:
Males solitary at shoot-tips; females in threes

Fruits:
Spiny, 4-lobed husk containing 3 small, triangular nuts

Lookalikes:
Beech (p.82)

Native to Chile and Argentina, and the S Hemisphere's equivalent of the more familiar Beech. The two trees are quite similar but, unlike its northern relative, Roble Beech is smaller and dislikes lime-rich soils. The leaves also turn brighter colours in autumn, being yellow or red. A remarkably fast-growing tree and increasingly planted for timber and ornament.

Evergreen
Up to 25 m

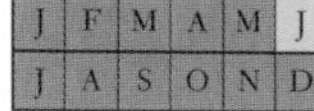

Evergreen Oak

Quercus ilex

ID FACT FILE

CROWN:
Broadly domed

BARK:
Almost smooth

LEAVES:
Alternate, 3–7 cm, leathery, densely white- or green-hairy beneath, entire or with short, spiny teeth

FRUITS:
Acorn a third to a half enclosed in cup 12 mm across. Cup-scales close-pressed, felted

LOOKALIKES:
Hollies (pp.157–158)

This is one of several evergreen species of oak. Leaves on low branches are spiny like Holly, probably as a defence against browsing by animals. Leaves produced higher up the tree and out of reach of animals have no spines. Native to the Mediterranean region, and originally part of the ancient evergreen forests once extensive there, Evergreen Oak is often planted elsewhere but does not grow well in very cold regions.

Evergreen
Up to 35 m

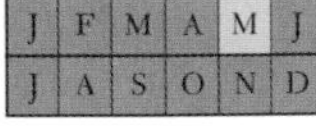

Lucombe Oak

Quercus × pseudosuber

ID FACT FILE

CROWN:
Usually dense

BARK:
Pale, ridged and corky or smoother and darker

LEAVES:
Alternate, 6–12 cm, lobed half-way to middle

FRUITS:
Acorn 25 mm, half enclosed in cup. Scales at base of cup spreading

/A natural hybrid between the evergreen Cork Oak and the deciduous Turkey Oak and intermediate between the parents. The semi-evergreen leaves stay on the tree except in very cold winters and are like those of Turkey Oak but less deeply lobed. The bark can resemble that of either parent. Lucombe Oak arose in 1762 in Lucombe's Nursery in Exeter and is now quite a common park tree.

Deciduous
Up to 35 m

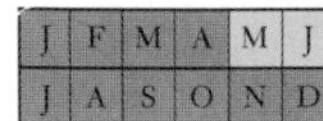

Turkey Oak

Quercus cerris

ID FACT FILE

Crown:
Wide-spreading

Bark:
Blackish, cracking into plates

Leaves:
Alternate, 5–10 cm, narrow lobes in 4–7 pairs, rough above, woolly beneath

Fruits:
Acorn a half to a third enclosed in cup 15–22 mm across. Cup-scales thick, curved outwards

A native of S Europe, widely planted and naturalised in many other areas. Typical of many deciduous oaks, Turkey Oak forms a large, spreading tree. Growth is not only rapid but is maintained over many years, with trees still flourishing after 200 or more years. The acorn cups are often described as 'mossy', from the resemblance of their narrow, pale green scales to mosses.

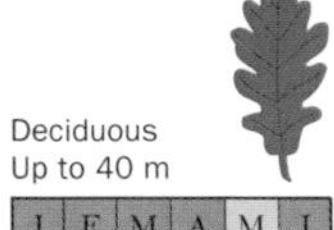

Deciduous
Up to 40 m

Sessile Oak

Quercus petraea

ID FACT FILE

Crown: Domed, spreading

Bark: Purplish-grey, smooth

Leaves: Alternate, 7–12 cm, 5–8 pairs of rounded lobes, hairy beneath and with reddish tufts in angles of veins

Fruits: Acorns in usually stalkless clusters. Acorn cup shallow, 12–18 mm across. Cup-scales thin, downy

A major forest tree, often found growing with the similar Pedunculate Oak. Sessile Oak has a straighter trunk and a less spreading crown. The acorns are borne in stalkless clusters, hence the name (sessile = stalkless). The bark was formerly much in demand for tanning and trees were frequently coppiced. Like many oaks, this species supports a variety of wildlife, especially insects.

Deciduous
Up to 45 m

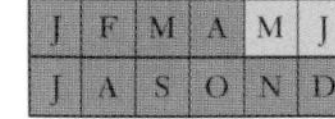

Pedunculate Oak

Quercus robur

Sometimes called English Oak, this species is typically the dominant tree of deciduous woodlands, especially on heavy clay soils in lowland regions. It is a massive tree with a broad, spreading crown and can live to a great age, up to 800 years. The first growth of leaves is often badly attacked by insects and a second growth, appearing reddish when young, may be produced in summer.

ID FACT FILE

Crown: Very large, spreading

Bark: Dark grey, deeply furrowed

Leaves: Alternate, 10–12 cm, lobes irregular, in 5–7 pairs

Fruits: Acorns in clusters on a long stalk. Acorn cup 11–18 mm across. All but tips of cup-scales fused together

Deciduous
Up to 35 m

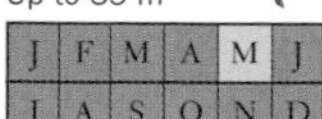

J	F	M	A	M	J
J	A	S	O	N	D

Red Oak

Quercus rubra

ID FACT FILE

Crown:
Broadly domed.

Twigs:
Dark red

Bark:
Silvery, smooth

Leaves:
Alternate, 12–22 cm, lobes reaching half-way to middle and with slender teeth

Fruits:
Acorn cup very shallow, 15–25 mm across. Cup-scales thin with fine hairs

This eastern N American species is now widely grown in Europe for its splendid autumn colours. The leaves, which have lobes tipped with slender teeth, turn a dark, vibrant red in autumn and contrast with the silvery colour of the bark. The best colours are found in young trees which are often grown planted along roads; old trees produce more yellows and browns.

Deciduous
Up to 25 m

J	F	M	A	M	J
J	A	S	O	N	D

Scarlet Oak

Quercus coccinea

ID FACT FILE

Crown:
Open, domed

Bark:
Grey-brown, smooth when young

Leaves:
Alternate, 9–15 cm, lobes spreading, toothed, in 3–4 pairs

Fruits:
Acorn half enclosed in cup 15–20 mm across. Cup-scales close-pressed

Closely resembling Red Oak but with more deeply lobed leaves, Scarlet Oak also comes from eastern N America and produces similarly brilliant autumn colours. These start with the shiny green leaves of one or two branches changing colour, then spreading until the whole crown is bright red or crimson. Scarlet Oak is also frequently planted along roads and in parks.

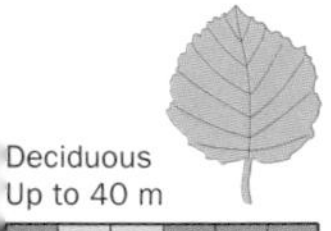

Deciduous
Up to 40 m

J	F	M	A	M	J
J	A	S	O	N	D

Wych Elm

Ulmus glabra

ID FACT FILE

Crown:
Very broad, spreading

Bark:
Greyish, smooth, becoming ridged

Leaves:
Alternate, 10–18 cm, stiffly hairy above, softer beneath, unequal base has one side curved over stalk

Flowers:
Purplish clusters appearing before leaves

Fruits:
Papery discs 15–20 mm long with a centrally placed seed

Elms are easily recognised by their papery, winged seeds and by their leaves in which the blade extends further down the midrib on one side than on the other. Wych Elm is native to much of Europe and is probably the commonest species remaining in Britain following the outbreak of Dutch Elm disease to which it is slightly resistant. However it does not produce suckers so affected trees cannot regenerate.

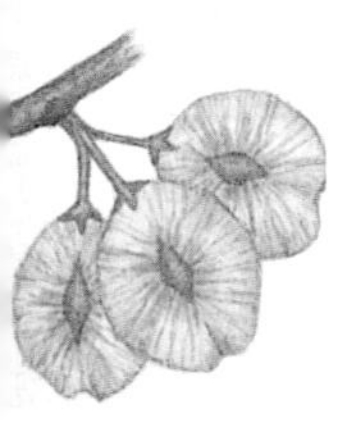

Deciduous
Up to 36 m

J	F	M	A	M	J
J	A	S	O	N	D

English Elm

Ulmus procera

ID FACT FILE

Crown: High, rather narrow.

Twigs: Densely hairy

Bark: Dark brown, grooved

Leaves: Alternate, 5–8 cm, stiffly hairy, base unequal

Flowers: Greenish clusters appearing before leaves

Fruits: Papery discs 10–17 mm with seed placed near top edge

English Elm is probably best known in Britain but also occurs in W and S Europe, growing along hedgerows and the edges of woods. Trees rarely produce seed, spreading by means of suckers instead. It was once a source of fine-quality timber but, like Dutch Elm, was badly affected by the outbreak of Dutch Elm disease and is now a rare tree.

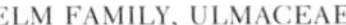

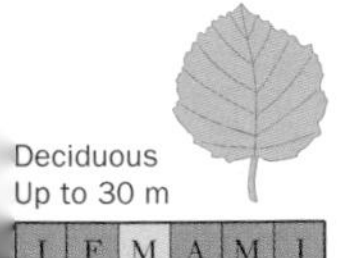

Deciduous
Up to 30 m

J	F	M	A	M	J
J	A	S	O	N	D

Small-leaved Elm

Ulmus minor

ID FACT FILE

Crown:
Narrow, branches angled upwards

Twigs:
Often with well-developed, corky wings

Leaves:
Alternate, 6–8 cm, smooth on both sides, long side of unequal base turned abruptly to join stalk

Flowers:
Reddish clusters appearing before leaves

Fruits:
Papery disc 7–18 mm long with seed placed near top edge

Small-leaved Elm is native throughout much of Europe and is a very variable species. Local populations of trees are sufficiently distinct from each other to be given different names such as Cornish Elm, Coritanian Elm and Jersey Elm. They are sometimes regarded as forming separate species but are very difficult to tell apart.

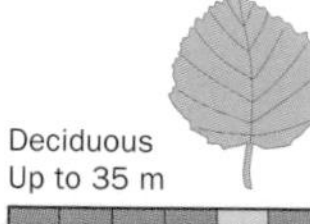

Deciduous
Up to 35 m

J	F	M	A	M	J
J	A	S	O	N	D

European White Elm

Ulmus laevis

ID FACT FILE

CROWN:
Tall, spreading

BARK:
Smooth, becoming ridged

LEAVES:
Alternate, 6–13 cm with grey down beneath, base unequal

FLOWERS:
Reddish clusters appearing before leaves

FRUITS:
Papery discs 10–12 mm long, fringed with white hairs; seed centrally placed

Distinguished from other elms by the extremely unequal leaf-bases and by the fringe of white hairs around the papery wing of the seed. The long-stalked, reddish flowers are noticeable in spring on the otherwise bare twigs. European White Elm grows in central and SE Europe and is sometimes planted to provide shelter but is rarely seen in Britain outside parks.

ELM FAMILY, ULMACEAE

Deciduous
Up to 30 m

J	F	M	A	M	J
J	A	S	O	N	D

Caucasian Elm

Zelkova carpinifolia

ID FACT FILE

Crown:
Ovoid. Branches almost erect

Bark:
Grey-brown, flaking to show orange patches

Leaves:
Alternate, 5–10 cm, stiffly hairy, slightly unequal and almost stalkless at base

Flowers:
Small; females in leaf-axils, males on bare lower part of twig

Fruits:
Ridged and nut-like, 5 mm

Despite its name this is not a true elm but belongs to a related genus. Caucasian Elm has a very distinctive shape, with a very short, squat trunk usually only 1–3 m high and a tall, broom-like crown with numerous, almost upright branches. Native to the Caucasus mountains, it is often planted in parks for its rich autumn colours. It is a slow-growing, long-lived tree.

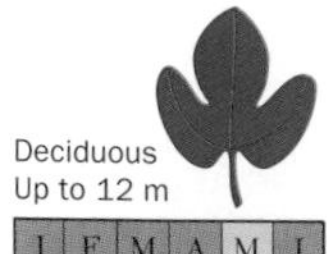

Deciduous
Up to 12 m

J	F	M	A	M	J
J	A	S	O	N	D

Black Mulberry

Morus nigra

ID FACT FILE

Crown:
Branches twisted

Twigs:
Hairy with milky latex

Trunk:
Often leaning

Leaves:
Alternate, 6–20 cm, toothed or lobed, roughly hairy above, soft beneath

Flowers:
Male and female catkins on same tree

Fruits:
2–2.5 cm, dark red or purple

Black Mulberry is not native to Europe but was introduced from Asia in ancient times and has become widely naturalised. It is grown for its edible fruits which resemble large raspberries and, in this species, are very dark red or purplish. They are very tart unless fully ripe. Great quantities of fruit are produced and often stain the ground under the tree where they have fallen.

Deciduous
Up to 8 m

J	F	M	A	M	J
J	A	S	O	N	D

Fig

Ficus carica

ID FACT FILE

Bark:
Pale grey, smooth

Leaves:
Alternate, 10–20 cm with 3–5 broad lobes, leathery, bristly

Flowers:
Minute, borne within hollow, pear-shaped structure

Fruits:
Large, fleshy, purplish when ripe

Fig trees are a characteristic feature of Mediterranean landscapes but will grow as far north as Britain, where they are often planted in sheltered gardens. The minute flowers are completely enclosed within a green, fleshy, pear-shaped structure. This gradually swells and takes on a purplish colour as it ripens fully in the second year to form the familiar fig.

Evergreen
Up to 20 m

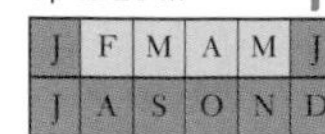

Sweet Bay

Laurus nobilis

ID FACT FILE

CROWN:
Bushy, dense

BARK:
Dull grey, smooth

LEAVES:
Alternate, 5–10 cm, leathery, margins wavy, aromatic when crushed

FLOWERS:
In small clusters, males and females on same tree; 4 petals

FRUITS:
Ovoid berries, ripening from green to black

Sweet Bay was the 'laurel' of victors' wreaths in classical times but is more familiar nowadays as a culinary flavouring used, for example, in bouquet garni. The leaves contain numerous aromatic oil glands which give off a pleasant scent when crushed. Native to the Mediterranean, Sweet Bay is not very hardy and in N Europe is often grown in pots as a small, clipped shrub.

Deciduous
Up to 3 m

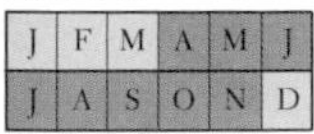

Witch Hazel

Hamamelis mollis

ID FACT FILE

Crown: Low, domed, spreading branches with tiny, star-shaped hairs when young

Leaves: Alternate, margins toothed, base unequal

Flowers: In clusters on bare twigs; 4 ribbon-like petals

Fruits: Capsule with exploding when ripe

Widely grown for its unusual flowers, which clothe the bare twigs well in advance of the leaves. The leaves, when they appear, resemble those of Hazel. All Asian species of Witch Hazel, including this one from China, are winter-flowering. American species are also commonly planted but are autumn-flowering. The bark and leaves are the source of witch hazel lotion used to treat bruises.

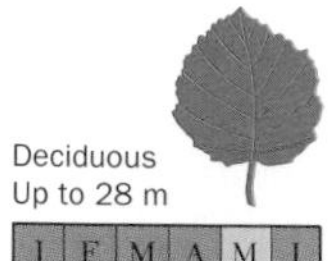

Deciduous
Up to 28 m

J	F	M	A	M	J
J	A	S	O	N	D

Sweet Gum

Liquidambar styraciflua

ID FACT FILE

Crown:
Conical

Bark:
Brown, fissured

Leaves:
Alternate, up to 15 cm, deeply 5-lobed, downy on veins beneath

Flowers:
Males in rounded clusters, females in globose heads; both sexes on same tree

Fruits:
Prickly, globose head of capsules

Lookalikes:
Maples (pp.148–152)

In its native N and Central America this tree provides the timber known as satinwood or satin walnut and a fragrant gum called storax which has medicinal uses. The leaves produce a similar fragrance when crushed. Frequent in parks in S and Central England, and in S Ireland. In Europe it is grown mainly as an ornamental tree because of the fine display of colours produced by the leaves in autumn.

MAGNOLIA FAMILY, MAGNOLIACEAE

Evergreen
Up to 30 m

J	F	M	A	M	J
J	A	S	O	N	D

Evergreen Magnolia

Magnolia grandiflora

ID FACT FILE

Crown:
Conical, branches spreading

Twigs:
Covered with thick, reddish down when young

Leaves:
Alternate, 8–16 cm, leathery, margins sometimes wavy, shiny above, rusty-hairy beneath

Flowers:
Solitary, up to 25 cm across, white, opening flat; petal-like segments 6

Fruits:
Borne in a narrow, cone-like structure 5–6 cm long

The Magnolias are not native to Europe but some species and numerous cultivars are grown as ornamentals. Many species are shrubby or dwarfed but this N American species makes a handsome tree in sheltered sites. Only a few extremely large, fragrant flowers appear on the tree at any one time, so the flowering period is prolonged. The flowers are initially conical but soon open fully.

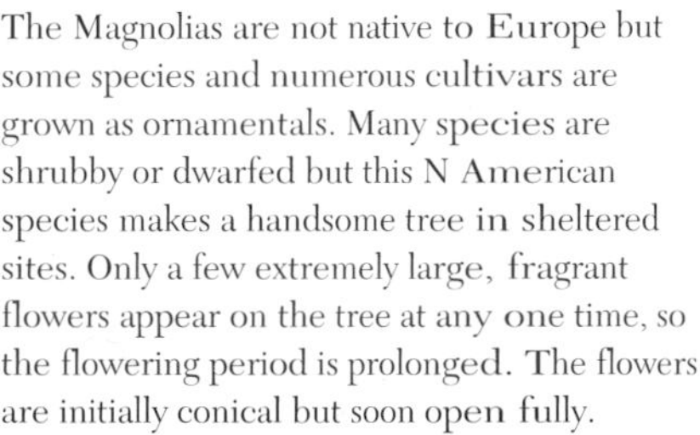

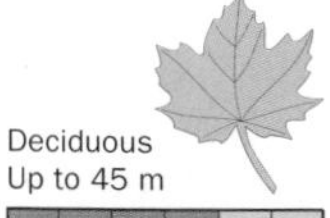

Deciduous
Up to 45 m

J	F	M	A	M	J
J	A	S	O	N	D

Tulip Tree

Liriodendron tulipifera

ID FACT FILE

Crown:
Columnar when young, becoming domed

Leaves:
Alternate, 7–12 cm, 1–3 spreading lobes per side. Apex notched or cut straight across. Bluish and waxy beneath

Flowers:
Large, cup-shaped with 9 petals, the inner 6 with a basal orange band

Fruits:
Narrow, cone-like

A tall, striking tree with distinctive leaves which look as though a piece has been snipped off the tips. When first open, the flowers are cup-shaped and resemble yellowish-green tulips. As they open further the resemblance diminishes but the flowers become more conspicuous as the brighter inner petals are revealed. Native to N America, it is grown in Europe for timber as well as ornament.

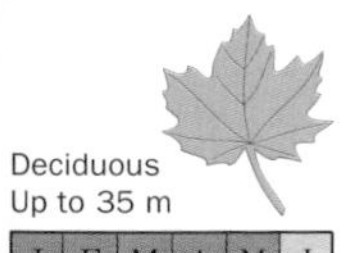

Deciduous
Up to 35 m

J	F	M	A	M	J
J	A	S	O	N	D

London Plane

Platanus × hispanica

ID FACT FILE

Bark:
Grey, flaking to show large yellow and buff patches

Leaves:
Alternate, up to 25 cm, lobed to less than halfway

Flowers:
In strings of globose heads; 2–6 male heads greenish, 2–5 females crimson

Fruits:
Brown, globose heads of plumed seeds

London Plane is a hybrid between the American and Oriental Planes. Possibly first appearing in Spain or S France and known since the 17th century, its exact origin is something of a mystery. It has now become one of the most popular and common street trees in Europe, especially in large towns where it tolerates high levels of air pollution.

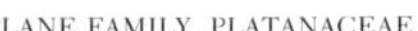

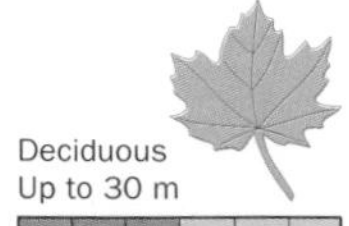

J	F	M	A	M	J
J	A	S	O	N	D

Oriental Plane

Platanus orientalis

ID FACT FILE

Crown:
Wide-spreading

Bark:
Like London Plane but duller

Leaves:
Alternate, up to 18 cm, lobed to more than half-way

Flowers:
In strings of globose heads like London Plane

Fruits:
Brown, globose heads of plumed seeds

Probably one of the parents of the more common London Plane and very similar to i Oriental Plane has leaves with deeper, narrower lobes, more numerous flowerhead each cluster and rather less colourful bark. I native to the Balkan Peninsula and Crete bu often planted in parks in other regions.

Deciduous
Up to 20 m

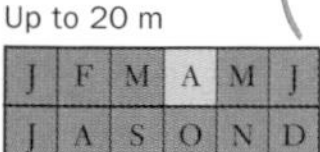

Common Pear

Pyrus communis

ID FACT FILE

CROWN:
Narrow

TWIGS:
Spiny in older trees

LEAVES:
Alternate, 5–8 cm, toothed, densely hairy at first

FLOWERS:
In clusters appearing with the leaves; 5 petals

FRUITS:
4–12 cm, pear-shaped to globose, sweet-tasting or sour

Common Pear was probably first introduced to Europe from W Asia and is now naturalised and widespread in woods and hedgerows. Solitary trees, however, are often the only surviving remnants of the gardens of old, abandoned houses. All of the orchard trees grown for their edible fruits, of which there are many different types, belong to the variety *culta*.

Deciduous
Up to 20 m

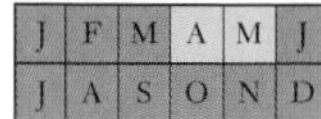

Wild Pear

Pyrus pyraster

ID FACT FILE

CROWN:
Rounded. Branches spreading, spiny

LEAVES:
Alternate, 2.5–7 cm, variable in shape, toothed near tip, hairy when young

FLOWERS:
In clusters of 4–5; 5 petals, crinkled

FRUITS:
1–3.5 cm, variable in shape

Very similar to Common Pear, Wild Pear is a bushier, more spiny tree and produces small, hard fruits which can ripen yellow, brown or black. The fruits are not always pear-shaped and can be top-shaped or almost globular like an apple but are easily identified by their characteristic, gritty-textured flesh. Wild Pear occurs throughout much of Europe, usually as single trees.

Deciduous
Up to 10 m

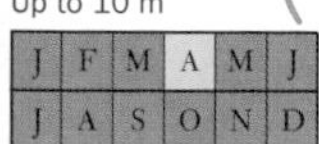

J	F	M	A	M	J
J	A	S	O	N	D

Willow-leaved Pear

Pyrus salicifolia

ID FACT FILE

CROWN:
Domed, often weeping

BARK:
Silvery

LEAVES:
Alternate, 3.5–9 cm, narrow, silvery-downy, upper surface becoming glossy green

FLOWERS:
In tight clusters; 5 petals, sometimes notched

FRUITS:
2.5 cm, pear-shaped or cylindrical, sour

A slender tree with willow-like leaves and a silvery overall appearance which makes it a popular ornamental in parks and gardens. The most commonly seen form is a variety in which the twigs and smaller branches are weeping. The fruits are too sour to be edible. Willow-leaved Pear is native to Asia, from Siberia south to the Caucasus Mountains and Iran.

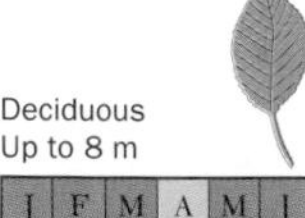

Deciduous
Up to 8 m

J	F	M	A	M	J
J	A	S	O	N	D

Plymouth Pear

Pyrus cordata

ID FACT FILE

Crown:
Branches spreading

Twigs:
Spiny, purplish

Leaves:
Alternate, 2.5–5.5 cm, margins toothed, often hairless even when young

Flowers:
In slender clusters appearing with leaves; 5 petals

Fruits:
Small, pear-shaped, ripening shiny red

Plymouth Pear makes a small tree at best, and is often no more than a spreading shrub. It is a rather rare species found from SW England and W France to the Iberian Peninsula. It is immediately distinguished from other pears by the small, long-stalked fruits which are dotted with warty, brown lenticels and do not retain the crown of withered sepals at the tip.

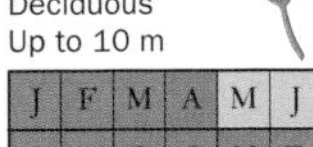

Deciduous
Up to 10 m

J	F	M	A	M	J
J	A	S	O	N	D

Crab Apple

Malus sylvestris

ID FACT FILE

CROWN:
Dense

TWIGS:
Often spiny

LEAVES:
Alternate, 3–11 cm, hairless on both sides

FLOWERS:
3–4 cm across, in clusters. Persistent sepals hairy on inner surface; 5 white or pink petals

FRUITS:
2.5–3 cm, hard, sour

Crab Apples are the ancestors of the cultivated apples. They were themselves once domesticated as fruit trees and introduced to many areas before falling out of use. The hard, sour fruits are still sometimes used for jellies and jams. Truly wild trees are spiny and have almost white flowers. The descendants of domesticated trees are unarmed and have pinkish flowers.

Deciduous
Up to 15 m

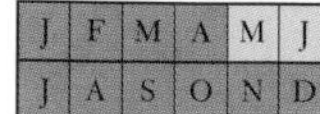

Cultivated Apple

Malus domestica

ID FACT FILE

Twigs: Downy, without spines

Leaves: Alternate, 4–13 cm, sparsely hairy above, downy beneath

Flowers: In clusters. Persistent sepals densely hairy on outside; 5 petals, usually pink, sometimes white

Fruits: Usually more than 5 cm, sweet-tasting

This is one of the most common orchard trees, grown in all but the hottest and coldest parts of Europe and sometimes becoming naturalised. It is a complex hybrid, derived from several wild species of apple including the Crab Apple. Cultivated apples are divided into thousands of varieties which differ in appearance and in the eating, cooking and keeping qualities of the fruits.

Deciduous
Up to 9 m

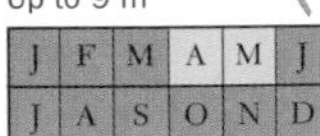

Japanese Crab Apple

Malus × floribunda

ID FACT FILE

CROWN:
Rounded

TWIGS:
Young twigs reddish and densely hairy

LEAVES:
Alternate, 4–8 cm, sometimes lobed, downy beneath when young

FLOWERS:
In abundant clusters; sepals deciduous; 5 petals, pink to white

FRUITS:
2.5 cm, globular, ripening bright yellow

Various flowering crab apples are now planted in Europe and Japanese Crab Apple is one of the most common. It is thought to be a garden hybrid and is not found anywhere in the wild. It produces so much blossom that the flowers hide the leaves in spring. The fragrant flowers are red or dark pink in bud but change colour to pale pink on opening and fade to white. The small yellow apples are not used for eating.

Deciduous
Up to 7.5 m

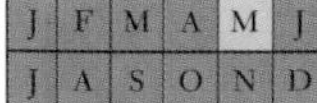

Quince

Cydonia oblonga

The Quince originates in Asia but has long been cultivated in Europe and is often naturalised. Quince is related to both apples and pears and its fruits can superficially resemble either. However, quinces are hard and woody even when ripe and have a distinctive, sweet fragrance. The fruits of wild trees do not generally exceed 3.5 cm but those of cultivated plants can be up to 12 cm long.

ID FACT FILE

Twigs:
Spiny, woolly when young, hairless later

Leaves:
Alternate, 5–10 cm, oval, grey-woolly beneath

Flowers:
4–4.5 cm, solitary, cup-shaped, pink or white

Fruits:
Variable in size and shape, usually large and globose or pear-shaped, downy, yellow

Deciduous
Up to 6 m

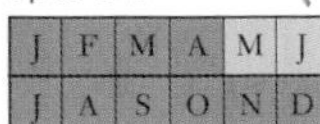

Medlar

Mespilus germanica

ID FACT FILE

Twigs:
Densely white-hairy when young

Leaves:
Alternate, 5–15 cm, dull green, crinkled and sometimes with toothed margins, very densely white-hairy beneath

Flowers:
3–6 cm across, solitary. Narrow, green sepals much longer than broad, white petals

Fruits:
2–3 cm, brown, with a hollow ringed by persistent sepals at apex

Medlar is a woodland tree native to SE Europe and naturalised in western and central areas. It was formerly much cultivated as a fruit tree and in some areas still is so. The fruits resemble large, dull brown rose-hips and stay on the tree until after the leaves have fallen. They are inedible until frost causes the flesh to begin to rot in a process known as 'bletting'.

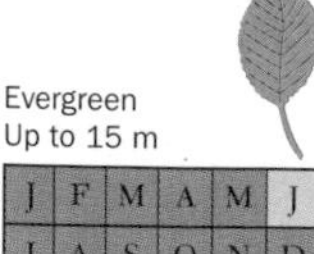

Himalayan Tree Cotoneaster

Cotoneaster frigidus

Most cotoneasters are shrubs, some of them low and creeping, but Himalayan Tree Cotoneaster is one of the few species to form a tree. It is generally evergreen, only shedding its leathery leaves if the winter weather is severe. The clusters of bright red fruits are also retained well into winter unless eaten by birds. Native to the Himalayas but planted in parks and gardens.

ID FACT FILE

Crown:
Of wide-arching branches

Leaves:
Alternate, spiralled around young twigs, in 2 ranks on older growth, 6–12 cm, elliptical, leathery. Grey- or white-woolly hairs beneath gradually lost

Flowers:
About 8 mm across, numerous, in flat clusters 5 cm across; 5 petals, white

Fruits:
Berries 5 mm, globose, bright red with a crown of persistent sepals

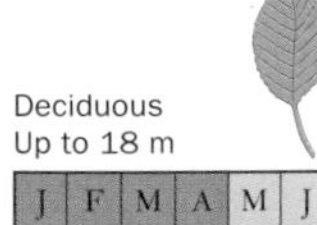

Deciduous
Up to 18 m

J	F	M	A	M	J
J	A	S	O	N	D

Hawthorn

Crataegus monogyna

ID FACT FILE

Bark:
Grey to brown, cracking into plates

Twigs:
Numerous thorns up to 15 mm

Leaves:
Alternate, shiny, 1.5–4.5 cm, ovate but deeply divided into usually 5–7 lobes

Flowers:
8–15 mm across, white or pink with 1 style

Fruits:
7–14 mm, dark or bright red; 1 seed

Hawthorns are perhaps best known as hedgerow shrubs and have been used for this purpose since hedges were first planted in Europe. They provide a quick-growing barrier to animals and their thorny twigs protect them from browsing. Hawthorn hedges come into leaf earlier and are denser than other hedges and support a greater variety of wildlife than any other. Left uncut, Hawthorns form sturdy, densely crowned trees.

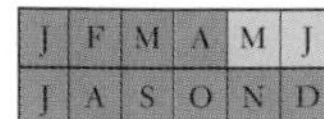

Deciduous
Up to 10 m

J	F	M	A	M	J
J	A	S	O	N	D

Midland Hawthorn

Crataegus laevigata

ID FACT FILE

Twigs:
With few thorns

Leaves:
Alternate, shiny, 1.5–6 cm, ovate with lobes usually reaching less than half-way to middle

Flowers:
15–24 mm, white, with 2–3 styles

Fruits:
15–24 mm, deep red; 2 seeds

More tolerant of shade than its relative the Hawthorn, Midland Hawthorn is more often found as a woodland tree, particularly in oak woods on damp, heavy soils. It also has fewer thorns and the fruits contain two seeds instead of one. The seeds are dispersed by birds which eat the fruits. The flesh of the fruit is digested but the hard seed passes harmlessly through the bird's body.

Deciduous
Up to 10 m

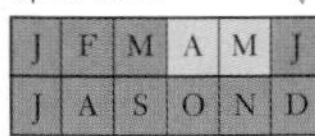

Juneberry

Amelanchier lamarkii

ID FACT FILE

CROWN:
Slender, open

TWIGS:
Shaggily white-hairy when young

LEAVES:
Alternate, up to 8 cm, oblong to elliptical. Margins slightly upturned

FLOWERS:
In clusters, stalks hairy. Petals white, narrow and erect

FRUITS:
1 cm, purplish-black with pale bloom, crowned with withered sepals

Juneberries are a group of mainly American shrubs and small trees. They produce drifts of white blossom in spring followed by edible fruits which appear, appropriately, from June to about August. They are much sought after by animals, birds and humans. This species is thought to be a natural hybrid which arose in the wild and was later introduced to Europe where it is widely planted for ornament and is naturalised in places.

Deciduous
Up to 20 m

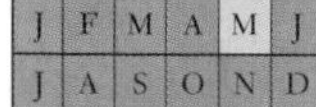

True Service Tree

Sorbus domestica

ID FACT FILE

Buds:
Rounded, green

Leaves:
Alternate, pinnate, leaflets in 6–8 pairs, 3–5.5 cm, toothed towards tip, softly hairy beneath

Flowers:
In domed clusters; 5 petals, white or creamy

Fruits:
2 cm or more, green or brown, sour

True Service Tree is native to dry woods in S Europe but naturalised elsewhere after its introduction as a fruit tree. It can be separated from the similar Rowan by differences in the buds, the fruits and the shape of the flowerheads. The fruits can be apple- or pear-shaped and can be mistaken for small, extremely sour pears. Like pears they are edible, but only after they have been frosted.

Deciduous
Up to 20 m

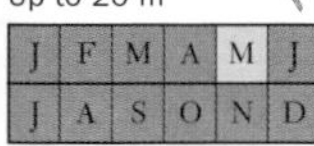

Rowan

Sorbus aucuparia

ID FACT FILE

BUDS:
Pointed, purple

LEAVES:
Alternate, pinnate, leaflets in 5–10 pairs, 3–6 cm, towards the tip, grey-hairy beneath

FLOWERS:
White, in flat-topped clusters

FRUITS:
6–9 mm, globose, scarlet

Sometimes called Mountain Ash, Rowan is common in upland areas, though it will grow at any altitude. Formerly used as a charm against many forms of witchcraft, its major modern use is as an attractive ornamental whose narrow shape makes it ideal as a street tree. Its fruits are avidly eaten by birds and will attract them even into town centres in winter.

Deciduous
Up to 14 m

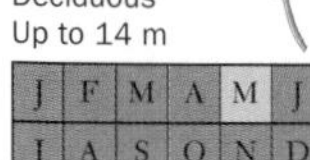

J	F	M	A	M	J
J	A	S	O	N	D

Hupeh Rowan

Sorbus hupehensis

ID FACT FILE

Leaves: Alternate, pinnate, leaflets bluish-green, in 5–6 pairs, 3.5–7.5 cm, sharply toothed towards tips; stalk reddish

Flowers: White, in flat-topped clusters

Fruits: 6 mm, globose, white or pale pink

Native to the mountains of Hupeh Province in W China where it was discovered early this century, Hupeh Rowan is widely planted in Europe as an ornamental tree. It closely resembles Rowan and grows equally well in the polluted air of towns. The bluish-green leaves turn bright red in autumn and the striking, pale fruits remain on the bare branches well into winter.

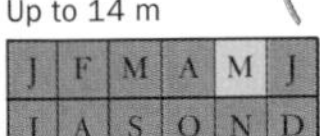

Deciduous
Up to 14 m

J	F	M	A	M	J
J	A	S	O	N	D

Bastard Service Tree

Sorbus hybrida

ID FACT FILE

CROWN:
Ovoid, dense

LEAVES:
Alternate, 7.5–10.5 cm, grey-green above, grey- or white-woolly beneath, pinnately divided into 2–4 pairs of leaflets but with a large lobed blade at the tip

FLOWERS:
White, in branched clusters

FRUITS:
10–12 mm, globose, red and speckled with small warts

The peculiar leaves of Bastard Service Tree appear intermediate in form between those of Rowan, which are pinnately divided and those of Whitebeam, which are undivided. Despite its name *hybrida* however, it is not a hybrid but a true species found in woodlands in SW Scandinavia and sometimes planted elsewhere as a hardy ornamental.

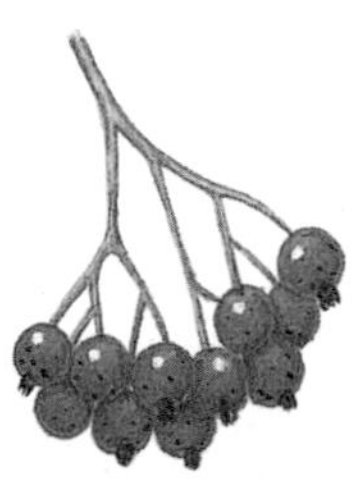

Deciduous
Up to 25 m

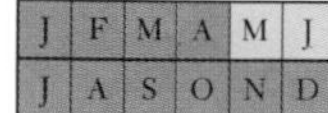

Wild Service Tree

Sorbus torminalis

ID FACT FILE

Crown:
Domed

Leaves:
Alternate, 5–10 cm, with 3–5 pairs of deep, toothed lobes, almost hairless

Flowers:
White, in branched clusters. Stalks woolly

Fruits:
12–18 mm, widest above the middle. Brown, with numerous speckles

Lookalikes:
Maples (pp. 148–152)

Wild Service Tree often grows in deciduous woodland and its presence is a good indication that a wood is very old. It has become rarer in Europe as these ancient woods have been reduced. The tree changes colour very early in autumn and stands out from its surroundings. The name 'The Chequers' found on many public houses in Britain reflects the former use of the fruits to make a drink of this name.

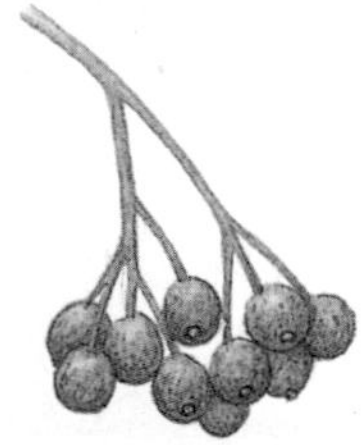

Deciduous
Up to 15 m

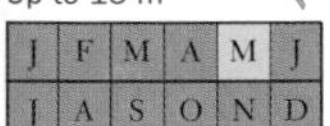

Swedish Whitebeam

Sorbus intermedia

ID FACT FILE

CROWN:
Domed. Trunk usually short

LEAVES:
Alternate, 6–12 cm, yellowish-grey hairs beneath. Lobes deepest at base of leaf-blade, becoming shallower towards tip with very thick

FLOWERS:
White, in flat-topped clusters

FRUITS:
12–15 mm, ovoid, scarlet with few speckles

Many of the whitebeams have northerly distributions and Swedish Whitebeam is native to Scandinavia and the Baltic. It is commonly planted elsewhere and is well adapted for use as a street tree, being small and compact, with hairy leaves to reduce water loss. The pale colour of the leaves protects them from light reflected from pavements and buildings.

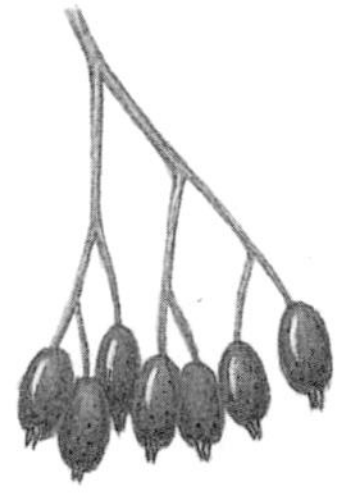

Deciduous
Up to 25 m

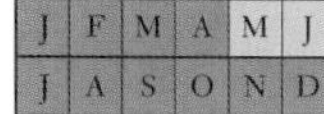

Whitebeam

Sorbus aria

ID FACT FILE

Crown:
Domed. Branches upswept

Leaves:
Alternate, 5–12 cm, oval, margins irregularly toothed, upper side bright green, lower densely white-hairy

Flowers:
White, in branched clusters

Fruits:
8–15 mm, ovoid, scarlet, with numerous small speckles

Lookalikes:
Wayfaring Tree (p.183)

Whitebeam is most noticeable in spring when the pale undersides of the leaves give the whole crown a silvery-white appearance. It can be identified among other, darker, trees from a considerable distance at this time of year. Whitebeam grows mainly in limestone areas in most of Europe but only in mountains in the south. It is often used as a street tree.

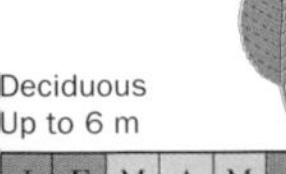

Deciduous
Up to 6 m

J	F	M	A	M	J
J	A	S	O	N	D

Peach

Prunus persica

ID FACT FILE

CROWN:
Bushy. Branches straight

LEAVES:
Alternate, 5–15 cm, lance-shaped but folded lengthwise to form a V, finely toothed

FLOWERS:
Single, in angle between leaf-bud and stem, appearing as leaf-buds open; 5 petals, dark pink, rarely pale pink or white

FRUITS:
4–8 cm, globular, downy

Probably originating in China, the Peach has been grown in Europe since ancient times for its luscious fruit and is a major commercial crop. It is not a hardy tree and in northern areas requires some protection, often being trained as a flat fan against a wall. The Nectarine is a cultivar which produces smooth-skinned fruits.

Deciduous
Up to 8 m

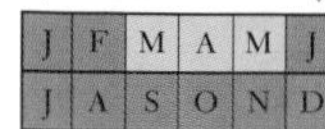

Almond

Prunus dulcis

ID FACT FILE

CROWN:
Open. Branches angled upwards, sometimes spiny

LEAVES:
Alternate, 4–13 cm, lance-shaped and folded lengthwise to form a shallow V, finely toothed

FLOWERS:
Paired, in angle between leaf-bud and stem, appearing before leaves open; 5 petals, pale pink, rarely white

FRUITS:
3.5–6 cm, flat-tened, grey-green, velvety

Like the Peach, the Almond has been grown in Europe since ancient times but probably originated in W Asia. The Almond also resembles the Peach in having velvety-skinned fruits but the flesh is very thin and it is the large stone with its edible kernel which is valued. The pale pink or white flowers appear very early in spring and Almonds are often grown as purely ornamental trees, especially in northern areas.

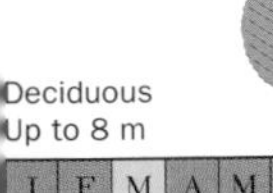

Deciduous
Up to 8 m

J	F	M	A	M	J
J	A	S	O	N	D

Cherry Plum

Prunus cerasifera

ID FACT FILE

CROWN:
Rounded. Branches sometimes spiny

LEAVES:
Alternate, 4–7 cm, oblong to oval, tapering at base and tip, teeth small and rounded

FLOWERS:
Single, appearing before leaves; 5 petals, white or pale pink

FRUITS:
3.5 cm, globular, yellow or red

In the wild, Cherry Plum produces numerous suckers and quickly spreads to form thickets. This ability makes it a convenient plant for hedges and it is often planted for this purpose. It is also grown for its sweet, cherry-like fruits. A commonly seen form is one with red leaves and pinkish flowers which is grown as an ornamental tree. Cherry Plum is native to the Balkans.

Deciduous
Up to 6 m

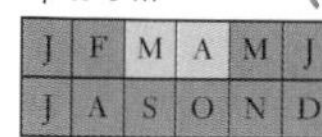

Blackthorn

Prunus spinosa

ID FACT FILE

CROWN:
Tangled. Branches black and spiny

LEAVES:
Alternate, 2–4.5 cm, oval, toothed, hairy on veins beneath

FLOWERS:
Numerous, appearing before leaves; 5 white petals

FRUITS:
1–1.5 cm, roughly globular, ripening blue-black with a grey, waxy bloom

A small tree, often forming dense thickets of shrubby growth from its numerous suckers. Blackthorn flowers in early spring and the drifts of white flowers stand out against the black twigs. A 'blackthorn winter' refers to one in which cold weather continues into the period when the tree is in flower. The small, acid fruits, called sloes, have a grape-like bloom.

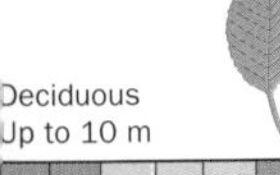

Deciduous
Up to 10 m

J	F	M	A	M	J
J	A	S	O	N	D

Wild Plum

Prunus domestica

ID FACT FILE

BRANCHES:
Straight, sometimes thorny

LEAVES:
Alternate, 3–8 cm, oval, toothed, dull green, smooth above, downy beneath

FLOWERS:
In clusters of 2–3, appearing with leaves; 5 white petals

FRUITS:
2–7.5 cm, colour ranging from greenish to red, purple or blue-black, sometimes with a waxy bloom

A complex hybrid between Blackthorn and Cherry Plum, Wild Plum includes several different fruit trees. The cultivated Plum has sparsely hairy and spineless twigs and large fruits. The cultivated Damson and Greengage and the wild Bullace all have densely hairy, spiny twigs and smaller fruits, those of Damson purple, those of Greengage yellow and those of Bullace red.

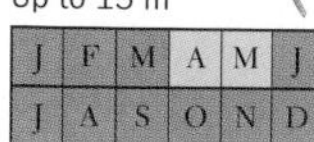

Deciduous
Up to 15 m

J	F	M	A	M	J
J	A	S	O	N	D

Japanese Cherry

Prunus serrulata

ID FACT FILE

Crown:
Sparse. Branches horizontal or fanning out from trunk

Bark:
Glossy, red- or purple-brown, banded

Leaves:
Alternate, 8–20 cm, oval, long-pointed and sharply toothed

Flowers:
In clusters of 2–4, appearing before leaves; 5 notched petals, white or pink

Fruits:
Up to 7 mm, dark reddish-purple

Probably native to China but introduced to Japan before being brought to Europe where it is a common suburban street tree and ornamental. There are numerous forms, some of them weeping or narrowly erect and differing in leaf and flower colour. The delicate flowers are often double, that is with two or more whorls of petals. Fruits are rarely produced by cultivated trees.

Deciduous
Up to 20 m

J	F	M	A	M	J
J	A	S	O	N	D

Spring Cherry

Prunus subhirtella

ID FACT FILE

Crown:
Dense, bushy

Twigs:
Crimson, downy

Leaves:
Alternate, 6 cm, oval, long-pointed, sharply and irregularly toothed. Veins and stalk downy

Flowers:
In clusters of 2–5, appearing before leaves; 5 petals, notched, pale pink

Fruits:
7–9 mm, purplish-black

Another of the many Japanese species of cherry which have been introduced to Europe, and one of the most widely planted. Like Japanese Cherry there are double-flowered and weeping forms of Spring Cherry as well as the more normal one. As the name suggests most trees flower in spring but some flower in autumn instead and are sometimes referred to as Autumn Cherry. All belong to the same species.

Deciduous
Up to 30 m

Wild Cherry

Prunus avium

ID FACT FILE

CROWN:
High, domed

BARK:
Red-brown, peeling in horizontal bands

LEAVES:
Alternate, 8–15 cm, oval to oblong, pointed, with sharp, forward-pointing teeth, veins with hairy tufts in angles

FLOWERS:
In clusters of 2–6, appearing just before leaves; 5 petals, 1–1.5 cm, white

FRUITS:
Up to 9–12 mm, usually dark red

Wild Cherry grows rapidly and attains a greater size than most other species of cherry. It is found wild in mixed and deciduous woods throughout most of Europe, especially in hilly regions, and is also grown for its fruit and timber. The fruits are usually dark red but range from yellowish to bright red or black and may be sweet or sour when ripe.

Deciduous
Up to 8 m

J	F	M	A	M	J
J	A	S	O	N	D

Sour Cherry

Prunus cerasus

ID FACT FILE

Crown:
Rounded

Bark:
Red-brown, peeling in bands

Leaves:
Alternate, leathery, 3–8 cm, oval, pointed, with small, blunt teeth. Downy beneath when young

Flowers:
Long-stalked, in clusters of 2–6, appearing just before leaves; 5 white petals

Fruits:
Up to 1.8 cm, bright red

Sour Cherry is similar to Wild Cherry but always has sour-tasting fruits. Because of their acidity these are used in cooking and for preserves. The reddish-brown bark of Sour Cherry is typical of many cherries. The horizontal bands peel easily and can become very shiny. Native to SW Asia, Sour Cherry is cultivated in much of Europe and has become naturalised in many areas.

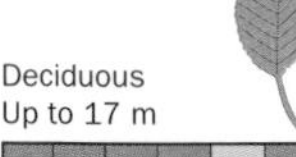

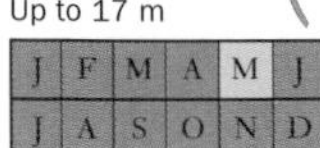

Bird Cherry

Prunus padus

ID FACT FILE

Bark:
Grey-brown, smooth, unpleasant-smelling

Leaves:
Alternate, slightly leathery, 6–10 cm, tapering at tip, finely toothed

Flowers:
Almond-scented, in spikes 7–15 cm long; 5 petals, 6–9 mm, white

Fruits:
6–8 mm, glossy black

Widespread except in the Mediterranean, Bird Cherry is somewhat similar to Wild Cherry and replaces that species in N Europe. It has few of the good features of Wild Cherry, making a smaller tree with unpleasant-smelling bark. The long, dense flower spikes are attractive but the black fruits are small and always very sour and acidic, even when fully ripe.

Deciduous
Up to 30 m

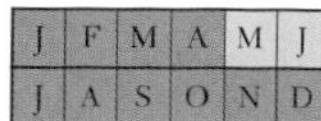

Rum Cherry

Prunus serotina

ID FACT FILE

CROWN: Spreading

BARK: Grey, smooth but peeling, aromatic

LEAVES: Alternate, 5–14 cm, tip tapering, fine teeth forward-pointing, shiny above, slightly downy beneath

FLOWERS: In spikes 7–15 cm long; 5 petals, 3–5 mm, white, margins minutely toothed

FRUITS: 6–8 mm, glossy black, sepals persisting at tip

Rum Cherry is a rather stout tree native to eastern N America. In Europe it is grown mainly for timber and occasionally as an ornamental. The bark is less colourful than in other cherries and has a bitter, aromatic scent. The bitter fruits are also unusual in being crowned with the withered remains of the persistent sepals, like an apple. Most cherries are completely smooth.

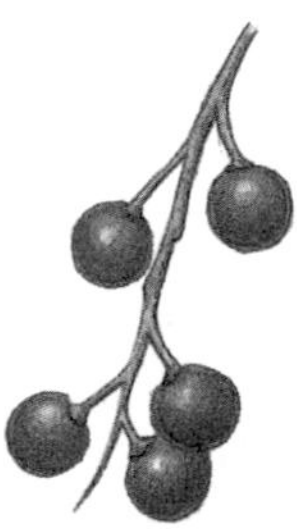

Evergreen
Up to 8 m

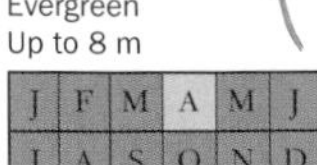

Cherry Laurel

Prunus laurocerasus

ID FACT FILE

Crown:
Spreading

Leaves:
Alternate, leathery, 10–20 cm, oblong, margin entire or minutely toothed and rolled under, shiny green above, yellowish beneath

Flowers:
Fragrant, in erect spikes 10–20 cm long; 5 petals, 4 mm, white

Fruits:
Globose, 2 cm, red ripening to glossy black

Cherry Laurel has a very laurel-like appearance and is, in fact, the plant most often used for so-called 'laurel' hedges. The glossy, evergreen leaves contain small amounts of cyanide and smell of bitter almonds when crushed. Introduced to many places from SE Europe, Cherry Laurel is widely naturalised in open woods but rarely flowers in deep shade.

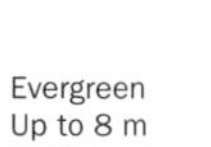

Evergreen
Up to 8 m

J	F	M	A	M	J
J	A	S	O	N	D

Portugal Laurel

Prunus lusitanica

ID FACT FILE

Twigs:
Red when young

Leaves:
Alternate, slightly leathery, 10–20 cm, elliptical, margin minutely toothed, dark, shiny green above, yellowish beneath. Stalk red

Flowers:
Fragrant, in long, erect spikes of up to 100 long; 5 petals, 4 mm, white

Fruits:
Ovoid to globose, ripening purplish-black

Superficially resembling Cherry Laurel, this evergreen is easily distinguished by its dark red twigs and leaf-stalks, toothed leaves and longer, looser spikes of flowers. Although native to the Iberian Peninsula and S France, it is quite hardy and is planted in many areas, sometimes becoming naturalised. In good conditions it can reach a height of 20 m, though this is exceptional.

Deciduous
Up to 15 m

J	F	M	A	M	J
J	A	S	O	N	D

Blackwood

Acacia melanoxylon

ID FACT FILE

Bark:
Brown, rough and furrowed

Leaves:
Alternate, 6–13 cm, narrow, blunt and slightly curved, leathery

Flowers:
Small, tubular, creamy-white, in clusters of globular heads each 10 mm across

Fruits:
Pods 7–12 cm, flattened and twisted

Blackwood is native to SE Australia and is one of several *Acacia* species introduced to Europe. Originally grown for timber which is used in veneers, it has become naturalised in south-western areas. The leaves are undivided and leathery but occasionally feathery. Pinnately divided leaves also appear, especially on young trees.

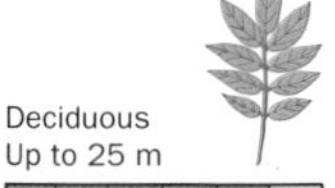

Deciduous
Up to 25 m

J	F	M	A	M	J
J	A	S	O	N	D

False Acacia

Robinia pseudoacacia

ID FACT FILE

CROWN:
Open

BARK:
With spiral ridges

LEAVES:
Alternate, 15–20 cm, pinnate, yellowish-green leaflets in 3–10 pairs. Stalk has 2 spines at base

FLOWERS:
Pea-like, white, fragrant, in hanging clusters

FRUITS:
Pods 5–10 cm

Native to N America but a popular garden and street tree in Europe. It may produce several trunks if the suckers which readily appear around the base are allowed to grow. Despite being large and showy, the flower clusters are often produced quite high in the crown and are easy to miss. However, the pods remain on the branches long after the leaves have fallen.

Honey Locust

Gleditsia triacanthos

Deciduous
Up to 45 m

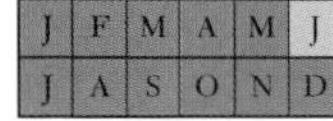

The Latin name for this species refers to the robust spines which usually grow in threes on twigs and branches. Those on the trunks, however, grow in larger clusters. They are very strong and sharp and provide formidable protection for the tree. Native to the Mississippi River basin, it is often grown in Europe although many of the trees planted in streets and parks are thornless varieties.

ID FACT FILE

Bark:
Brown, cracked vertically

Spines:
Large clusters on trunk and branches, in threes on twigs

Leaves:
Alternate; pinnate with leaflets 2–3 cm or twice pinnate with leaflets 8–20 mm; leaf always tipped with a spine

Flowers:
Small, in dense clusters; 5 greenish-white petals

Fruits:
Flattened, curved pods 30–45 cm

Deciduous
Up to 10 m

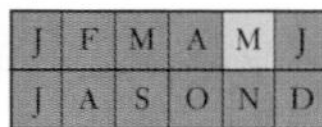

Judas Tree

Cercis siliquastrum

ID FACT FILE

Crown:
Spreading

Leaves:
Alternate, 7–12 cm, almost circular with heart-shaped base

Flowers:
Pea-like, deep pink, appearing with or before leaves in clusters on trunk and branches as well as on twigs

Fruits:
Pods 6–10 cm

A native of dry areas of the Mediterranean and traditionally the tree from which Judas Iscariot hanged himself. It blooms before the leaves unfold and is unusual in bearing flowers directly on the trunk and main branches as well as on the twigs. The Judas Tree is often planted for ornament further north where it thrives on chalky soils, but it is intolerant of cold weather.

Deciduous
Up to 7 m

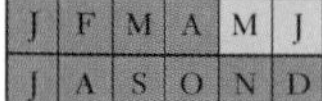

Laburnum

Laburnum anagyroides

ID FACT FILE

Crown:
Slender. Branches angled upwards or arching

Leaves:
Alternate, trifoliate, leaflets 3–8 cm, grey-green and silky-hairy

Flowers:
Pea-like, 2 cm, yellow, fragrant, in hanging clusters 10–30 cm long

Fruits:
Pods 4–6 cm, persisting on tree after splitting

Originally from central and S Europe, Laburnum is now planted and often naturalised throughout much of Europe. In its native habitat it grows in mountain woods and thickets. The pods are produced in large numbers and persist for some time on the tree. They are black on the outside but split to reveal the pale inner surface and the rows of dark, bean-like seeds which are highly poisonous.

Deciduous
Up to 7 m

J	F	M	A	M	J
J	A	S	O	N	D

Voss's Laburnum

Laburnum × watereri

ID FACT FILE

Crown:
Slender. Branches angled upwards or arching

Leaves:
Alternate, trifoliate, leaflets 3–8 cm, grey-green and only slightly hairy

Flowers:
Pea-like, 2 cm, yellow, fragrant, in hanging clusters 25–35 cm long

Fruits:
Pods 4–6 cm, but rarely produced

This tree is a hybrid between Laburnum and Scotch Laburnum and is somewhat intermediate between both. It has the longer, denser flower clusters of one parent and the early flowering period of the other and is a stronger, longer-lived tree than either. It also produces fewer of the poisonous seeds. Unknown in the wild, it is probably now the most commonly planted ornamental Laburnum.

Deciduous
Up to 15 m

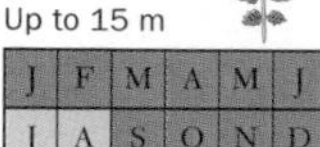

Golden Rain Tree

Koelreuteria paniculata

ID FACT FILE

Crown:
Trunk and branches stout but crown thin

Bark:
Cracked with orange layer beneath

Leaves:
Alternate, pinnate, leaflets 3–8 cm and deeply toothed or lobed at base

Flowers:
In large, branched clusters; 4 yellow petals

Fruits:
5.5 cm, conical, papery, with red veins

A species named for its large clusters of golden-yellow flowers. The fruiting capsules are unusual, becoming inflated and bladder-like with a papery texture as they ripen. They split by means of three valves to release the black seeds. Native to E Asia, Golden Rain Tree is grown as an ornamental and street tree in the warmer areas of Europe, as far north as Britain.

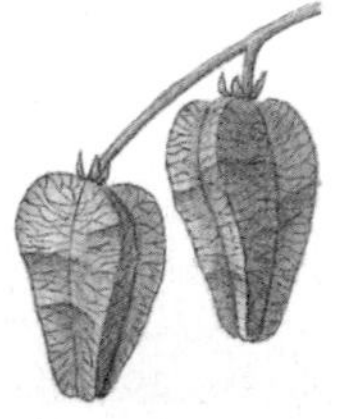

Deciduous
Up to 30 m

J	F	M	A	M	J
J	A	S	O	N	D

Tree of Heaven

Ailanthus altissima

ID FACT FILE

Crown:
Branches angled upwards

Bark:
Grey

Leaves:
Alternate, pinnate, leaflets 7–12 cm with 2–4 small teeth at base

Flowers:
In large branched clusters, fragrant; males and females on different trees; 5 greenish-white petals

Fruits:
3–4 cm, including twisted, membranous wing

Tree of Heaven can produce abundant suckers, some of them at considerable distances away from the main trunk. Such growth is particularly common in warm climates where the tree can spread rapidly, but is less marked in cooler regions. The leaves, which are red when unfolding, have a rank, sour smell when crushed. Native to China but resistant to atmospheric pollution and often planted in streets and town parks.

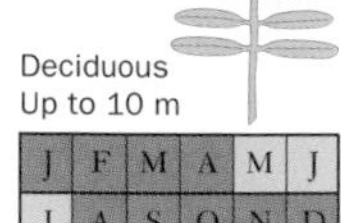

Stag's-horn Sumach

Rhus typhina

ID FACT FILE

CROWN:
Rounded

TWIGS:
Regularly forked, covered with dense, velvety hair when young

LEAVES:
Alternate, pinnate, drooping leaflets 5–12 cm, toothed, softly hairy

FLOWERS:
In dense, conical heads of 10–20 cm. Males greenish, females red, on different trees

FRUITS:
4 mm in diameter, nut-like, in hairy, dull crimson heads

A freely suckering tree which often produces several trunks. The curved, regularly forking branches are densely covered with hair when young and resemble a stag's new-grown antlers. Native to N America and widely grown as an ornamental since the leaves produce bright autumn colours and the reddish fruiting heads, found only on female trees, persist well into winter.

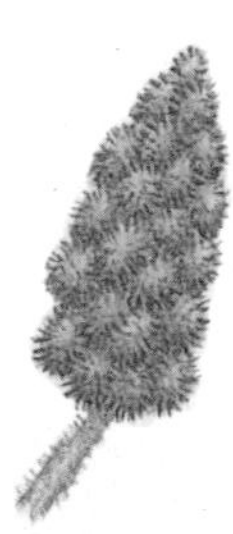

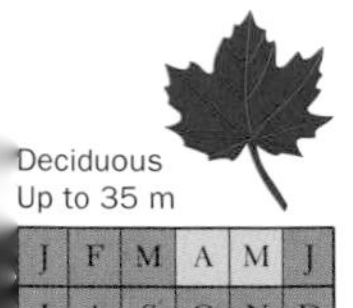

Deciduous
Up to 35 m

J	F	M	A	M	J
J	A	S	O	N	D

Sycamore

Acer pseudoplatanus

ID FACT FILE

Crown: Wide-spreading

Leaves: Opposite, 10–15 cm, the 5 spreading lobes coarsely toothed

Flowers: Appearing with the leaves, yellowish-green. Males and females in separate, hanging clusters

Fruits: Joined at the base in pairs 3.5–5 cm long, the wings forming a right-angle

Sycamores are fast-growing, invasive trees which rapidly colonise new areas. The winged seeds can be carried over considerable distances by the wind and they germinate easily. The leaves of rapidly growing young trees are deeply lobed, those of old, slower-growing trees are more shallowly divided. The largest of the European maples, and native or naturalised in most areas.

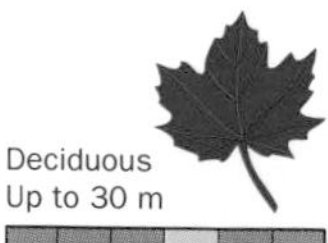

J	F	M	A	M	J
J	A	S	O	N	D

Norway Maple

Acer platanoides

ID FACT FILE

CROWN:
Spreading

LEAVES:
Opposite, 10–15 cm, 5–7 spreading lobes with slender teeth

FLOWERS:
Appearing with the leaves. Males and females in separate, erect clusters

FRUITS:
Paired, 3.5–5 cm long, yellowish, the wings horizontal or forming a wide angle

Norway Maple is a native tree in much of Europe, especially in the north where it is very hardy. A dark red-leaved form is often planted in streets and parks. Norway Maple produces a very sweet sap and trees are often attacked by squirrels which strip and eat the bark and the sap beneath. Very similar to Sycamore but generally smaller and with erect, not pendulous, flower-clusters.

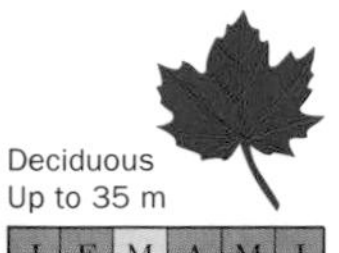

Deciduous
Up to 35 m

J	F	M	A	M	J
J	A	S	O	N	D

Silver Maple

Acer saccharinum

ID FACT FILE

CROWN:
Tall, spreading

BARK:
Greyish, smooth but becoming shaggy

LEAVES:
Opposite, 9–16 cm, 5 deep lobes irregularly toothed. Silver-hairy beneath

FLOWERS:
Reddish; males and females in separate clusters; petals absent

FRUITS:
Paired, 5 cm long, wings making a narrow angle

Silver Maple is one of several sugar-producing species originating from N America. The sweet sap is tapped daily for about six weeks in early spring and, after processing, yields maple syrup which can be refined into sugar. In Europe it is planted as an ornamental for its silvery leaves and attractive shape. The fruits, which are shed in late spring of the following year, rarely ripen in Europe.

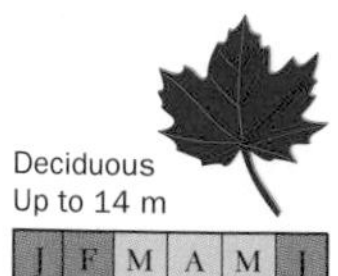

Deciduous
Up to 14 m

J	F	M	A	M	J
J	A	S	O	N	D

Red Maple

Acer rubrum

ID FACT FILE

Twigs:
Reddish

Bark:
Grey, smooth when young, becoming rough

Leaves:
Opposite, 5–20 cm, with 3–5 shallow, toothed lobes. Silvery-white beneath

Flowers:
Usually red. Males and females in separate, short clusters

Fruits:
Red, paired, wings making a narrow angle

An aptly named tree which has red twigs, spring buds, young leaves, flowers and fruits. The autumn foliage is a mixture of rich yellows and striking reds. The rich colours are due to the high sugar content of the leaves. Native to N America but widely planted for ornament in Europe. It has a marked preference for damp soils and the roots can be troublesome, growing into underground drains and clogging them.

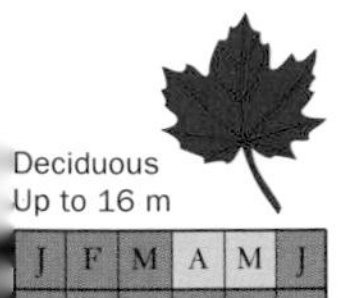

Deciduous
Up to 16 m

J	F	M	A	M	J
J	A	S	O	N	D

Smooth Japanese Maple

Acer palmatum

ID FACT FILE

CROWN:
Domed

BARK:
Brown, smooth

LEAVES:
Opposite, 7–9 cm, with 5–7 deep, narrow, sharply toothed lobes

FLOWERS:
Dark purplish, in erect clusters

FRUITS:
Reddish, paired, wings making a wide angle

One of the smallest of the maples and often seen as a shrub or dwarf tree with a short, twisted trunk. Native to Japan and very variable in the wild. Many cultivars are also grown, differing mainly in the colour and degree of lobing of the leaves. Two forms are commonly planted as park trees and ornamentals in Europe, one with purple leaves, the other with leaves turning scarlet in autumn.

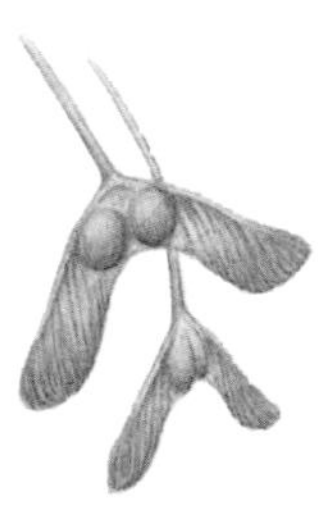

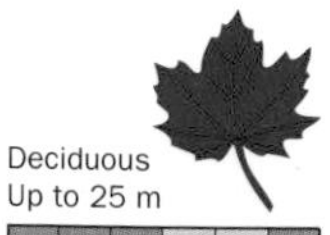

Deciduous
Up to 25 m

J	F	M	A	M	J
J	A	S	O	N	D

Field Maple

Acer campestre

ID FACT FILE

Crown:
Rounded

Twigs:
Often with corky wings

Leaves:
Opposite, 4–12 cm, 3 lobes themselves further lobed or with rounded teeth towards tips

Flowers:
Yellowish-green, in erect clusters appearing with leaves; 5 petals

Fruits:
Paired, 2–4 cm long, wings horizontal

A common tree in N Europe. Many of the largest specimens have been felled for their timber, known as bird's-eye maple, and mostly smaller specimens remain. Trees that are pruned regularly, such as those growing in hedgerows, may develop broad, corky wings along the twigs. Despite the leathery texture of the leaves, Field Maple is deciduous, the leaves turning butter-yellow in autumn before falling.

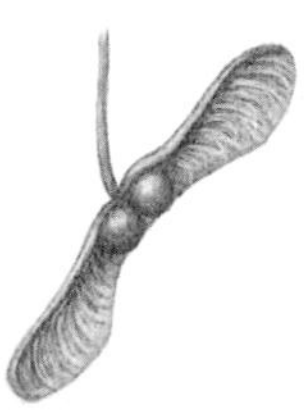

Box-elder

Acer negundo

ID FACT FILE

CROWN:
Irregular

TRUNK:
Short, often with swellings

LEAVES:
Opposite, 10–15 cm, pinnate with 5–7 toothed leaflets

FLOWERS:
Appearing before leaves; males red, females green, on different trees; petals absent

FRUITS:
Paired, 2 cm long, wings making a narrow angle

LOOKALIKES:
Ashes (pp.176–177)

Most species of maple have palmately divided leaves but Box-elder has pinnate leaves resembling those of an ash and is sometimes called Ash-leaved Maple. It is easily distinguished from ashes by the winged fruits which are borne in pairs, not singly. Native to eastern N America. A form with yellow and green variegated leaves is commonly planted in Europe and is sometimes naturalised.

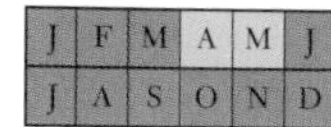

Deciduous
Up to 35 m

J	F	M	A	M	J
J	A	S	O	N	D

Horse-chestnut

Aesculus hippocastanum

ID FACT FILE

Crown:
Wide-spreading

Twigs:
Red-brown, with large, sticky winter buds

Leaves:
Opposite, palmate; 5–7 toothed leaflets each 10–25 cm long

Flowers:
2 cm across, in erect, conical spikes; 4–5 petals, frilly, stamens protruding

Fruits:
Up to 6 cm, spiny husk enclosing shiny brown seeds

This large, spreading tree is native to the Balkan mountains but has been introduced to many other parts of Europe. It is commonly planted in broad avenues and parks. The spiny fruits contain 1–3 shiny brown seeds – the familiar conkers – which germinate readily, so the tree is often naturalised. Horse-chestnut is easily recognised in winter by its very sticky buds which may be up to 3.5 cm long.

Deciduous
Up to 30 m

J	F	M	A	M	J
J	A	S	O	N	D

Red Horse-chestnut

Aesculus × carnea

ID FACT FILE

CROWN:
Spreading

TWIGS:
Red-brown, with large, sticky winter buds

LEAVES:
Opposite, palmate; 5 leaflets, toothed, drooping

FLOWERS:
Like those of Horse-chestnut but pink or red instead of white

FRUITS:
Up to 6 cm, husk spineless, seeds shiny brown

American species of Horse-chestnut are called Buck-eyes, from the resemblance of the seeds to an eye-ball. Red Horse-chestnut is a hybrid of garden origin between the European Horse-chestnut and the Red Buck-eye of North America, and is often planted as an ornamental tree. The naturally drooping leaves give the trees the appearance of constantly suffering from the effects of drought.

Evergreen
Up to 5 m

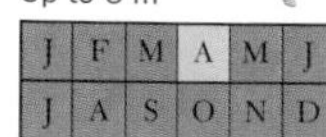

Box

Buxus sempervirens

ID FACT FILE

Twigs:
4-angled, green with white hairs

Leaves:
Opposite, leathery, 1.5–3 cm, oblong to oval with notched tip, margins rolled under

Flowers:
Tiny clusters consist of 5–6 males around a single female; petals absent

Fruits:
Woody capsule about 7 mm with 3 spreading horns at tip, blue-green ripening to brown

Box is best known as a garden shrub used for topiary, in which the bushes are clipped into a variety of shapes. It is also used for clipped hedges although Box hedges nowadays have been largely superseded by Privet. In its native habitat of dry, chalky soils Box can form a good-sized tree but it is becoming rare in the wild. The horned capsules split explosively when ripe, flinging the seeds considerable distances.

Evergreen
Up to 15 m

J	F	M	A	M	J
J	A	S	O	N	D

Holly

Ilex aquifolium

Holly is very tolerant of shade and often forms a shrubby understorey in woods where other small trees cannot survive. An old tradition that it was unlucky to cut hollies means that many are still seen growing as single trees in otherwise well-trimmed hedgerows. Berries are only produced by female trees and are a favourite winter food for birds, especially thrushes.

ID FACT FILE

CROWN:
Conical

BARK:
Silver-grey, smooth

LEAVES:
Alternate, 5–12 cm, waxy, stiff and leathery. Wavy margins with spines

FLOWERS:
Up to 6 mm, in small clusters; males and females on separate trees; 4 petals white

FRUITS:
Berries 7–12 mm diameter, scarlet

Evergreen
Up to 20 m

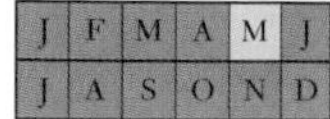

Highclere Holly

Ilex × altaclarensis

ID FACT FILE

Crown: Domed

Bark: Purple-grey, smooth

Leaves: Alternate, to 9 cm, waxy, leathery. Flat margins entire or with a few weak spines

Flowers: Up to 12 mm, in small clusters, males and females on separate trees; 5 white petals

Fruits: Berries 12 mm diameter, scarlet

Not all species of Holly have spiny foliage. Highclere Holly is a hybrid between prickly-leaved Holly and the unarmed Canary Holly. It has intermediate leaves, usually with a few weak spines along the margins. It is a vigorous and pollution-resistant tree, with many variegated and golden-leaved cultivars. These are widely planted for ornament in towns and seaside regions.

Deciduous
Up to 6 m

J	F	M	A	M	J
J	A	S	O	N	D

Spindle Tree

Euonymus europaeus

ID FACT FILE

Twigs:
4-angled when young

Leaves:
Opposite, 3–10 cm, oval with tapering tip. Margins toothed

Flowers:
In inconspicuous clusters; 4 narrow, greenish-yellow petals

Fruits:
Pink, 4-lobed capsule 1–1.5 cm

Spindle Trees are common on lime-rich soils but are inconspicuous for much of the year as the leaves have few distinguishing features and the flowers are small and greenish. They are much more noticeable in autumn when the leaves turn dark red and the fruits ripen. The peculiarly shaped capsules have four distinct lobes and are matt pink. Each lobe splits to reveal a single orange seed.

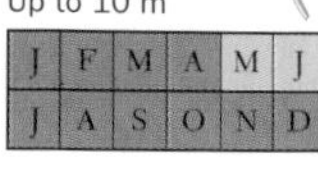

Deciduous
Up to 10 m

J	F	M	A	M	J
J	A	S	O	N	D

Buckthorn

Rhamnus catharticus

ID FACT FILE

Branches:
At right-angles

Leaves:
Opposite, crowded on short side-twigs which end in a spine, 3–7 cm, oval with 2–4 pairs of curved veins

Flowers:
In small clusters, fragrant, males and females on separate trees; 4 narrow, greenish petals

Fruits:
Berries 6–8 mm in diameter, black

Buckthorn produces two kind of shoots: long shoots which bear widely separated pairs of leaves and extend the tree's growth, and short side-shoots which bear crowded leaves and the inconspicuous flower-clusters. Dense clusters of attractive-looking black berries are produced by female trees. They are a violent laxative, hence the tree's alternative name, Purging Buckthorn.

Deciduous
Up to 5 m

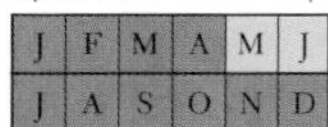

Alder Buckthorn

Frangula alnus

A small tree, often no more than a shrub, found on acid soils. The leaves characteristically hang downwards on the twigs as they change colour in autumn. The berries are green when immature and turn yellow, then red before ripening to black. Despite its name, Alder Buckthorn is not related to Alder but does grow in similar, marshy conditions. It is common in much of Europe.

ID FACT FILE

Branches:
Opposite, angled upwards

Leaves:
Mostly opposite, 2–7 cm, widest above middle, with 7–9 pairs of curved veins, margins entire, wavy

Flowers:
Small, in clusters; 5 greenish-white petals

Fruits:
Berries 6–10 mm in diameter, purple-black

Deciduous
Up to 11 m

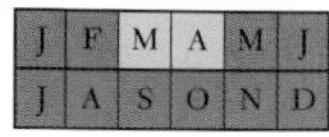

Sea Buckthorn

Hippophae rhamnoides

Sea-buckthorn is confined to seaside places, on cliffs, dunes and sand-bars. In these exposed sites it seldom reaches its full height, instead forming sprawling shrubs stunted by the wind. All parts of the tree are covered with minute, silvery scales which are easily rubbed off. These are too small to see with the naked eye but give a distinctive silvery cast to the whole tree.

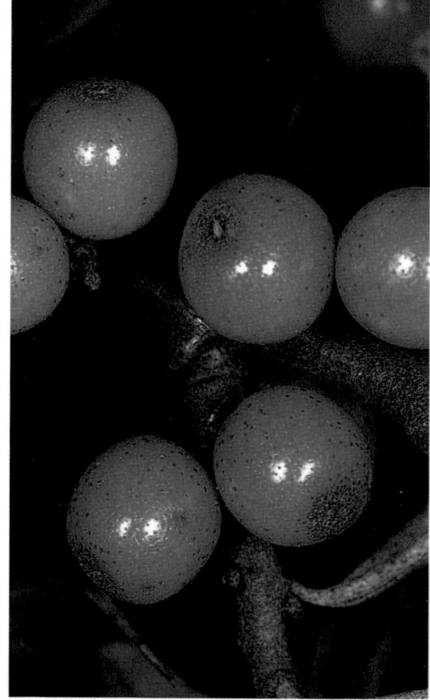

ID FACT FILE

Bark:
Blackish

Twigs:
Thorny, silvery when young

Leaves:
Alternate, 1.6 cm long but only 3–10 mm wide. Silvery on both sides or dull grey-green above

Flowers:
Greenish, appearing before leaves; males and females on separate trees; tubular with 2 sepals, petals absent

Fruits:
Berries 6–8 mm, oval, orange

Deciduous
Up to 8 m

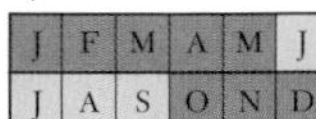

Tamarisk

Tamarix gallica

ID FACT FILE

Crown:
Much-branched

Bark:
Dark purple

Leaves:
Alternate, 1.5–2 mm, scale-like

Flowers:
Slender spikes 1.5–4.5 cm long, borne in clusters; petals 1.5–2 mm, pink or white but soon falling

Fruits:
Brown capsule; seeds with a plume of white hairs

A slender, rather shrubby tree with unusual, feathery foliage. The leaves are reduced to tiny scales to reduce water-loss in the dry coastal habitats where the tree grows. The flowers are also tiny but are massed into slender spikes and produced so prolifically that the whole tree appears pinkish when in flower. The seeds are plumed with hairs, allowing them to be dispersed by the wind.

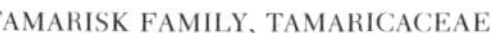

Deciduous
Up to 8 m

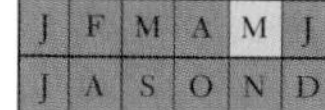

African Tamarisk

Tamarix africana

ID FACT FILE

Crown:
Much-branched

Bark:
Black

Leaves:
Alternate, 1.5–4 mm; scale-like, margins papery

Flowers:
In slender, solitary spikes 3–6 cm long; petals 2–3 mm, pink or white, persistent

Fruits:
Brown capsule; seeds with a plume of white hairs

Very similar to the closely related Tamarisk but with larger leaves and flowers; also found mainly in coastal areas, chiefly in SW Europe. Trees growing near the sea must be able to deal with the high levels of salt in their environment. One of the adaptations found in Tamarisks is the ability to excrete excess salt from special glands in their leaves.

Deciduous
Up to 32 m

J	F	M	A	M	J
J	A	S	O	N	D

Small-leaved Lime

Tilia cordata

ID FACT FILE

Crown:
Dense. Branches arching downwards

Leaves:
Alternate, 3–9 cm, heart-shaped, finely toothed, pale green beneath with reddish tufts of hairs in angles of veins

Flowers:
White, fragrant, hanging in a cluster beneath a pale greenish wing

Fruits:
Ribbed nuts 6 mm across

Native to limestone areas and chalky soils in most of Europe except the far north and south. Small-leaved Lime was probably the last tree species to reach Britain after the Ice-Age but before the formation of the English Channel. It was a characteristic tree of the original forests in lowland Britain but did not reach Ireland and cannot grow from seed in the cooler climate of Scotland.

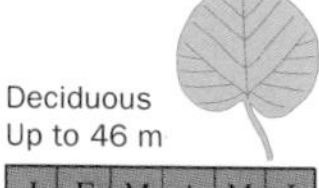

Deciduous
Up to 46 m

J	F	M	A	M	J
J	A	S	O	N	D

Common Lime

Tilia × vulgaris

ID FACT FILE

Crown:
Tall, narrow

Leaves:
Alternate, 6–10 cm, heart-shaped or flattened at base, finely toothed, dull green above, paler beneath with whitish tufts of hairs in angles of veins

Flowers:
Yellowish, fragrant, hanging in a cluster beneath a yellow-green wing

Fruits:
Nuts 8 mm, downy, slightly ribbed

A naturally occurring hybrid between Small-leaved Lime and Large-leaved Lime. Unusually for a hybrid, it can reproduce by seed. It was formerly one of the most frequently planted street trees but the leaves become infested with aphids which produce large amounts of partly digested sap or honeydew. This coats the leaves, as well as anything under the tree such as parked cars, making them sticky and unpleasant.

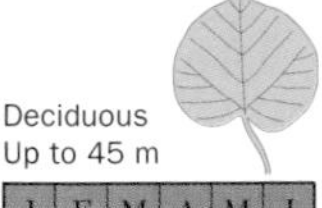

Deciduous
Up to 45 m

J	F	M	A	M	J
J	A	S	O	N	D

Caucasian Lime

Tilia × euchlora

Caucasian Lime is a hybrid between Small-leaved Lime and a rare species from the Crimea. It shares one parent with the more widespread Common Lime to which it is very similar. It is distinguishable by the darker leaves with reddish hairs beneath and the narrower, tapering nuts. It is mainly planted as a decorative and street tree in central Europe.

ID FACT FILE

Leaves: Alternate, 6–10 cm, heart-shaped or flattened at base, finely toothed, glossy green above, paler beneath with reddish tufts of hairs in angles of veins

Flowers: Yellowish, fragrant, hanging in a cluster beneath a yellow-green wing

Fruits: Nuts 6 mm, tapering at both ends, slightly ribbed

Deciduous
Up to 40 m

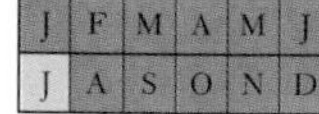

Large-leaved Lime

Tilia platyphyllos

ID FACT FILE

Crown:
Narrow, branches angled upwards

Leaves:
Alternate, 6–9 cm, heart-shaped, sharply toothed, hairy on both surfaces

Flowers:
Yellowish, fragrant, hanging in a cluster beneath a greenish-white wing

Fruits:
Nuts globular, 8–12 mm across with 3–5 ribs

This is the earliest-flowering of the Limes, producing blossom several weeks before other species. The flowers produce large quantities of nectar and bees, in particular, swarm around the trees, attracted to this rich food source. Sugars in the nectar can be poisonous in large quantities and the trees are often surrounded by dead or dying bees, especially bumble-bees.

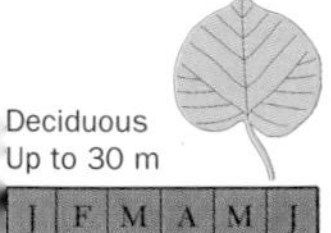

Deciduous
Up to 30 m

J	F	M	A	M	J
J	A	S	O	N	D

Silver Lime

Tilia tomentosa

ID FACT FILE

Crown:
Compact, rounded; young twigs white-hairy

Leaves:
Alternate, 8–10 cm, base heart-shaped but lopsided, sharply toothed, silvery-hairy beneath

Flowers:
Yellow or white, fragrant, hanging in a cluster beneath a yellowish wing

Fruits:
Ribbed nuts 6–12 mm long, downy

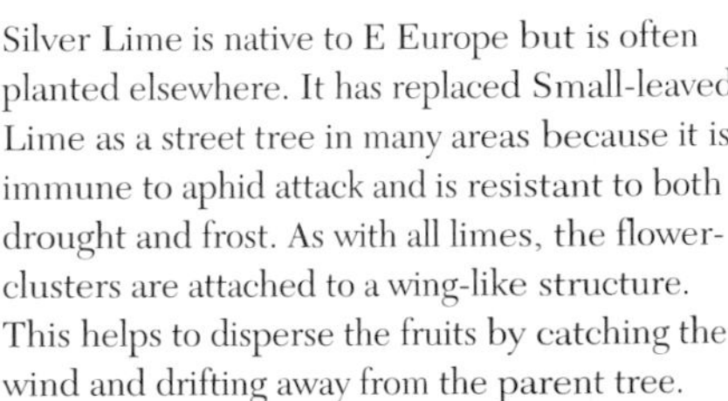

Silver Lime is native to E Europe but is often planted elsewhere. It has replaced Small-leaved Lime as a street tree in many areas because it is immune to aphid attack and is resistant to both drought and frost. As with all limes, the flower-clusters are attached to a wing-like structure. This helps to disperse the fruits by catching the wind and drifting away from the parent tree.

Deciduous
Up to 30 m

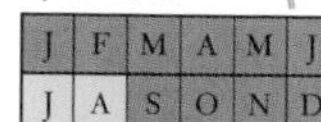

Weeping Silver Lime

Tilia petiolaris

ID FACT FILE

Twigs: Pendulous, young ones white-hairy

Leaves: Like those of Silver Lime but with long, drooping and silver-hairy stalks

Flowers: Yellow or white, fragrant, hanging in a cluster beneath a yellowish wing

Fruits: Nuts ribbed, downy

Weeping Silver Lime is a tree of unknown origin and so similar to Silver Lime that it may be simply an extreme form of that species. The pendulous branches and silvery leaves on long, drooping stalks make it an attractive and distinctive ornamental tree often seen in parks. Although it produces fruits, these are almost always sterile.

Cider Gum

Eucalyptus gunnii

Evergreen
Up to 30 m

J	F	M	A	M	J
J	A	S	O	N	D

Many *Eucalyptus* species have peeling or shredding outer bark. That of Cider Gum is typical, peeling to form a 'stocking' around the base of the trunk and leaving the pale, rather pastel-coloured inner bark exposed above. The flowers are also typical, with petals and sepals fused to form a pointed bud-cap which falls off when the flower opens. Cider Gum is planted as an ornamental in Europe.

ID FACT FILE

Bark:
Smooth, peeling except around base to leave trunk greenish-white or tinged pink

Leaves:
On young wood opposite, 3–4 cm, broadly oval, base clasping twig. On old wood alternate, narrower, up to 7 cm, grey-green

Flowers:
In clusters of 3 in leaf-axils; petals and sepals absent

Fruits:
About 1 cm, woody, opening by 3–5 teeth

Evergreen
Up to 15 m

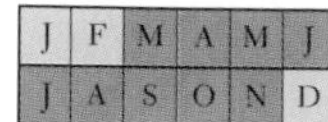

Snow Gum

Eucalyptus pauciflora subsp. *niphophila*

ID FACT FILE

Bark: Golden-brown to reddish, peeling to leave white patches

Leaves: On young wood opposite, up to 7.5 cm, elliptical, silvery-white. On old wood alternate, up to 10 cm, grass-green to bluish

Flowers: Bluish-green with red bud-caps, about 1 cm long, often warty; petals and sepals absent

Fruits: About 12 mm, cup-shaped, woody, opening by teeth

Snow Gum is one of the smallest of the Gums and also one of the hardiest. In Australia it grows in mountains at altitudes of around 1800 m, and can withstand both frost and snow. Its tolerance of cold enables it to survive in the cooler parts of Europe and it is often grown as an ornamental. Like those of most Gums, the leaves turn edgeways in strong sunlight so the tree casts little shade.

Deciduous
Up to 8 m

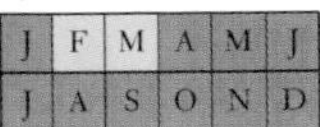

Cornelian Cherry

Cornus mas

ID FACT FILE

Crown:
Spreading

Leaves:
Opposite, 4–10 cm, oval to elliptical with prominent veins, yellowish-green

Flowers:
Appearing before leaves in clusters 2 cm across; 4 bright yellow petals

Fruits:
Berries cherry-like but rather oblong, 12–20 mm, bright red

Copious blossom appears before the leaves and turns this tree into a mass of yellow in late winter or early spring. When the leaves do appear they are also a distinctive yellowish-green with very prominent veins. The fruits resemble rather oblong, short-stalked cherries and are edible but somewhat tart, even when ripe. They are usually made into preserves.

Deciduous
Up to 12 m

Strawberry Tree

Arbutus unedo

ID FACT FILE

Bark:
Reddish, peeling in strips

Twigs:
Red when young

Leaves:
Alternate, 4–11 cm; the sharp, irregular teeth nearest apex red-tinged; stalk red

Flowers:
9 mm, urn-shaped with 5 small, rounded lobes, white or pink-tinged, in drooping clusters

Fruits:
2 cm across, globular, warty, deep, dull red

In autumn this species bears the current year's flowers alongside the previous year's fruits. The dull red, warty fruits scarcely resemble strawberries and, although edible, are not very palatable. Strawberry Tree has an unusual distribution. It is a Mediterranean species which also occurs on the fringes of W Europe northwards to Ireland, where it is thought to be a pre-Ice Age remnant.

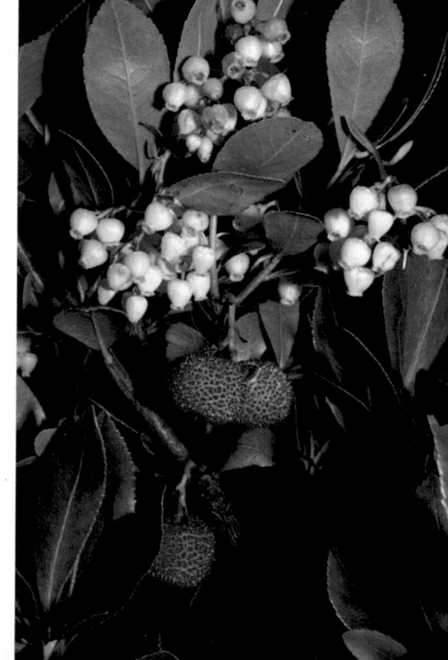

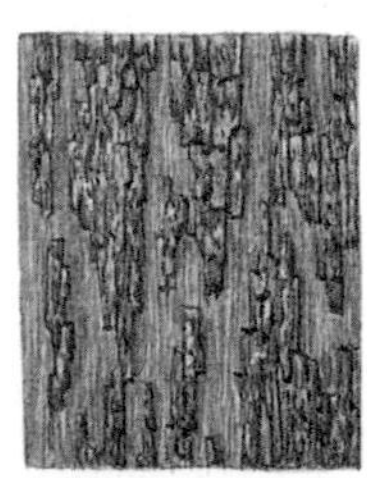

Evergreen
Up to 5 m

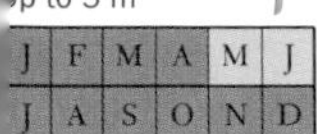

Rhododendron

Rhododendron ponticum

ID FACT FILE

CROWN:
Dense, rather spreading

LEAVES:
Alternate, 6–20 cm, elliptical, somewhat leathery, lacking teeth or hairs

FLOWERS:
In dense heads of 10–15; 4–6 cm across, bell-shaped with 5 spreading petals, mauve; 10 stamens protruding

FRUITS:
Capsule with many small seeds

Native to southern parts of Spain, Portugal and the Balkans, Rhododendron is a small tree or shrub which forms a dense understorey in woods on acid soils. It was introduced to Britain over 200 years ago to provide cover for game. Unfortunately it thrives almost too well in the mild British climate and has become an invasive weed in some areas, ousting less competitive native species.

Deciduous
Up to 40 m

J	F	M	A	M	J
J	A	S	O	N	D

Common Ash

Fraxinus excelsior

ID FACT FILE

Crown:
Domed, open

Bark:
Grey, smooth, becoming ridged with age

Winter buds:
Black

Leaves:
Opposite, pinnate, 7–13 leaflets each 5–12 cm, toothed. Midrib with white hairs beneath

Flowers:
Tiny, purplish, appearing before leaves in separate male and female clusters

Fruits:
2.5–5 cm, winged

A common and widespread tree of woodlands and hedgerows, preferring chalky or lime-rich soils. It is one of the later trees to come into leaf in the spring. Tiny flowers are wind-pollinated and lack sepals and petals. Males and females may be borne on separate trees or on separate branches of the same tree. Easy to identify in winter by the prominent black buds in opposite pairs.

Deciduous
Up to 24 m

J	F	M	A	M	J
J	A	S	O	N	D

Manna Ash

Fraxinus ornus

ID FACT FILE

Crown:
Domed

Bark:
Grey, smooth

Winter buds:
Grey or brown

Leaves:
Opposite, pinnate, 5–9 leaflets each 3–10 cm, toothed. Veins with white or brownish hairs beneath

Flowers:
Fragrant, in large clusters; 4 petals, 5–6 mm, narrow, white

Fruits:
1.5–2.5 cm, winged

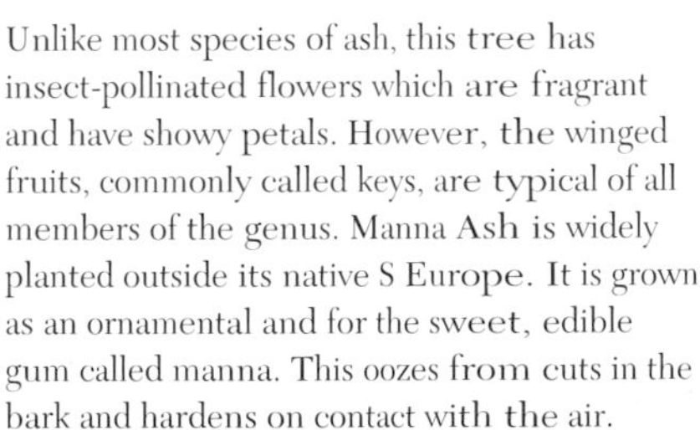

Unlike most species of ash, this tree has insect-pollinated flowers which are fragrant and have showy petals. However, the winged fruits, commonly called keys, are typical of all members of the genus. Manna Ash is widely planted outside its native S Europe. It is grown as an ornamental and for the sweet, edible gum called manna. This oozes from cuts in the bark and hardens on contact with the air.

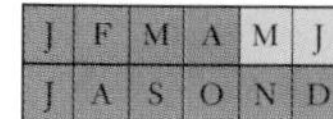

Deciduous
Up to 7 m

J	F	M	A	M	J
J	A	S	O	N	D

Lilac

Syringa vulgaris

ID FACT FILE

Crown:
Dense, twiggy

Leaves:
Opposite, 4–8 cm, oval or heart-shaped, often yellowish-green

Flowers:
Tubular with 4 spreading lobes, fragrant, in dense, conical heads 10–20 cm long, lilac or white

Fruits:
Brown capsule about 1 cm long

Lilacs sucker freely and will readily form tall, untidy shrubs or even twiggy thickets but can also grow as small trees with well-defined trunks. Native to rocky hills in the Balkan Peninsula, Lilac is commonly planted as an ornamental and is naturalised in many areas. In the wild the fragrant flowers are almost always lilac to purple but creamy-flowered and white forms are common in gardens.

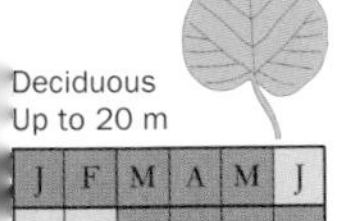

Deciduous
Up to 20 m

J	F	M	A	M	J
J	A	S	O	N	D

Indian Bean Tree

Catalpa bignonioides

ID FACT FILE

Crown:
Broadly domed

Bark:
Greyish, smooth, scaly with age

Leaves:
Opposite or in whorls of 3, 10–25 cm, heart-shaped at base, sometimes shallowly lobed

Flowers:
5 cm across, in conical clusters; 5 petals, frilly, white spotted with yellow and purple

Fruits:
Pendulous capsules 15–40 × 1 cm

Native to south-eastern N America but introduced to many parts of Europe and now a common sight in parks and town squares. The large, showy flowers resemble those of Horse-chestnut but are much larger. The large leaves open late and fall early so the tree is leafless for much of the year. However, the long, bean-like pods persist on the bare branches and are a distinctive autumn feature of this tree.

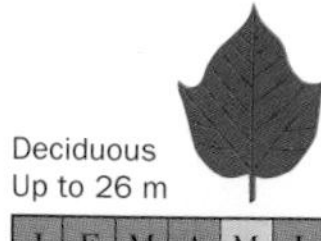

Deciduous
Up to 26 m

J	F	M	A	M	J
J	A	S	O	N	D

Foxglove Tree

Paulownia tomentosa

ID FACT FILE

Crown: Spreading, branches few

Twigs: Thick, purplish, warty

Leaves: Opposite, 45 cm, broad, heart-shaped, tip long and tapering. Densely grey-hairy beneath

Flowers: 6 cm long, in erect heads 20–30 cm long; tubular with 5 spreading lobes, violet

Fruits: Glossy, sticky, ovoid capsule, 5 cm

Native to China, introduced as an ornamental. The striking tubular flowers are violet on the outside and yellow within and resemble those of the Foxglove. The flower-buds, which are large and covered with brown hair, are formed in the autumn. They are conspicuous on the bare winter twigs and remain dormant until the following spring. This makes them vulnerable to bad weather which may destroy the buds long before flowering.

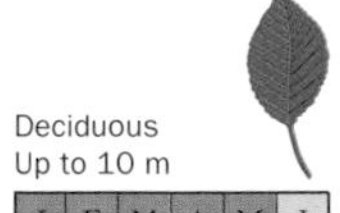

Elder

Sambucus nigra

ID FACT FILE

CROWN:
Branches curved outwards

BARK:
Pale brown, corky and deeply grooved

LEAVES:
Opposite, pinnate, 5–7 leaflets each 4.5–12 cm, sharply toothed

FLOWERS:
Fragrant, numerous in branched, flat-topped clusters 10–24 cm across; 5 white petals

FRUITS:
Berries 6–8 mm, black, whole cluster drooping when ripe

Elders are common on disturbed soil which is rich in nitrogen and grow quickly to form large shrubs or small trees. The leaves are rank smelling but the flowers are cloyingly sweet. The edible berries which follow are ripe when the heads droop. Both flowers and berries are rich in vitamin C and are collected for domestic and commercial use. All other parts of the plant are mildly poisonous.

Deciduous
Up to 4 m

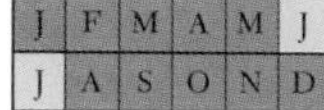

J	F	M	A	M	J
J	A	S	O	N	D

Guelder Rose

Viburnum opulus

ID FACT FILE

Twigs:
Angled, greyish, hairy

Leaves:
Opposite, 3–8 cm, with 3–5 spreading, toothed lobes

Flowers:
White, in circular heads 4.5–10.5 cm across with large sterile flowers around the rim and small fertile flowers in the centre; 5 petals

Fruits:
8 mm, scarlet, translucent

Lookalikes:
Maples (pp.148–152)

Found throughout most of Europe, Guelder Rose prefers damp habitats and is one of the few tree species to thrive in fenlands. The flowerheads have a ring of large, showy outer flowers surrounding much smaller and more numerous inner ones. The outer flowers are sterile but serve to attract pollinating insects to the fertile inner flowers. The bark, leaves and berries are all poisonous.

Deciduous
Up to 6 m

J	F	M	A	M	J
J	A	S	O	N	D

Wayfaring Tree

Viburnum lantana

ID FACT FILE

Twigs:
Cylindrical, grey, hairy

Leaves:
Opposite, 4–14 cm, oval, finely toothed, grey-green. Rough and hairy, especially beneath

Flowers:
In dense, domed heads 6–10 cm across; 5 white petals

Fruits:
8 mm, oval, red ripening black

Lookalikes:
Whitebeams (pp.123–124)

A common tree on downland, in thickets and scrub and along country tracks, especially on chalky or limestone soils. These are dry habitats and the dense hairs on the undersides of the leaves help to reduce water loss. The astringent berries are avidly eaten by birds. They ripen quickly but not simultaneously within a fruiting head so each one contains a mixture of red and black berries.

Evergreen
Up to 7 m

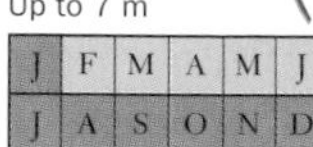

Laurustinus

Viburnum tinus

ID FACT FILE

CROWN:
Dense

LEAVES:
Opposite, 3–10 cm, narrowly to broadly oval, glossy above, margins entire

FLOWERS:
In domed clusters 4–9 cm across; 5 petals, pale pink on outside, white within

FRUITS:
8 mm, globular, blue

A very bushy evergreen, often only forming a tall shrub. Native to woods and thickets in the Mediterranean region but sufficiently hardy to thrive much further north. It is widely planted as an ornamental and frequently becomes naturalised. The main flush of flowers appears in winter but flowering may continue into summer. The distinctive fruits have a metallic sheen.

Evergreen
Up to 13 m

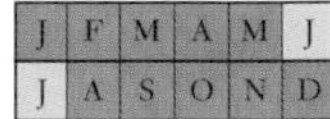

Cabbage Tree

Cordyline australis

ID FACT FILE

Crown:
Leaves in tufts at tip of trunk

Bark:
Greyish to brown, cracked into small squares

Leaves:
30-90 cm, sword-shaped, hard

Flowers:
Fragrant, in large, branched cluster 60-120 cm long growing from centre of crown; 6 petals white

Fruits:
Berries 6 mm, bluish-white

Lookalikes:
Palms (p.186)

Superficially palm-like in appearance but actually a member of the Agave family which also contains Yucca and Century Plant. The trunk only forks after flowering to give a branched effect. Young leaves are erect but older ones at the base of the tuft droop and partially obscure the trunk. Native to New Zealand but grown for ornament in sheltered areas.

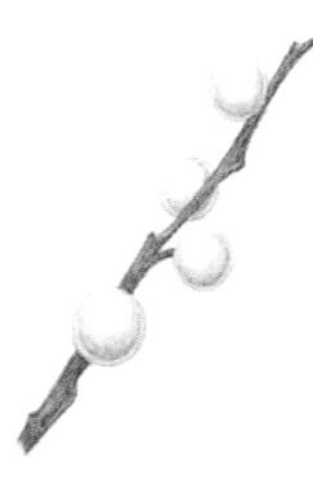

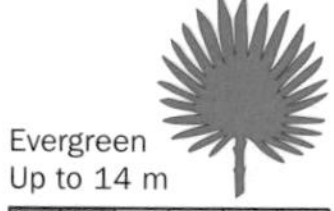

J	F	M	A	M	J
J	A	S	O	N	D

Chinese Windmill Palm

Trachycarpus fortunei

ID FACT FILE

Trunk:
Brown, shaggy

Leaves:
Up to 100 cm, fan-shaped or circular, divided into many slender, pleated segments. Long stalks fibrous at base

Flowers:
In clusters 70–80 cm long, yellow, fragrant; males and females on separate trees; 3 petals

Fruits:
2 cm, 3-lobed, purple-white

A tall palm with large, fan-shaped leaves. The old leaves are very persistent and obscure the very straight, unbranched trunk beneath the crown. Further down the trunk remains covered with the shaggy fibres of old leaf-bases, but it may be bare towards the base where these have worn away. Native to China and fairly tolerant of cold so planted in many parts of Europe, including coastal areas of Britain.

INDEX

Abies alba 11
  grandis 13
  nordmanniana 12
  procera 14
Acacia, False 139
Acacia melanoxylon 138
Acer campestre 152
  negundo 153
  palmatum 151
  platanoides 148
  pseudoplatanus 147
  rubrum 150
  saccharinum 149
Aesculus hippocastanum 154
  ×*carnea* 155
Ailanthus altissima 145
Alder, Common 74
  Grey 75
Almond 126
Alnus glutinosa 74
  incana 75
Amelanchier lamarkii 117
Apple, Crab 109
  Cultivated 110
  Japanese Crab 111
Araucaria araucana 46
Arbustus unedo 174
Ash, Common 176
  Manna 177
Aspen 69

Bay, Sweet 98
Bean-tree, Indian 179
Beech 82
  Roble 83
Betula pendula 77
  papyrifera 78
  pubescens 76
Birch, Downy 76
  Paper-bark 78
  Silver 77
Blackthorn 128
Blackwood 138
Box 156
Box-elder 153
Buckthorn 160
  Alder 161
Buxus sempervirens 156

Cabbage-tree 185
Carpinus betulus 79
Castanea sativa 81
Catalpa bignonioides 179
Cedar, Atlantic 39
  Japanese Red 45
  Pencil 55
  Western Red 47
Cedar-of-Lebanon 40
Cedrus atlantica 39
  deodara 38
  libani 40
Cercis siliquastrum 141
Chamaecyparis lawsoniana 49
  nootkatensis 51
  obtusa 48
  pisifera 50
Cherry, Bird 134
  Cornelian 173
  Japanese 130
  Rum 135
  Sour 133
  Spring 131
  Wild 132
Chestnut, Sweet 81
Cordyline australis 185
Cornus mas 173
Corylus avellana 80

Cotoneaster frigidus 114
Cotoneaster, Himalayan Tree 114
Crataegus laevigata 116
monogyna 115
Cryptomeria japonica 45
× *Cupressocyperis leylandii* 52
Cupressus macrocarpa 53
Cydonia oblonga 112
Cypress, Hinoki 48
Lawson 49
Leyland 52
Monterey 53
Nootka 51
Sawara 50

Deodar 38
Douglas-fir 24

Elder 181
Elm, Caucasian 95
English 92
European White 94
Small-leaved 93
Wych 91
Eucalyptus gunnii 171
pauciflora subsp. *niphophila* 172
Euonymus europaeus 159

Fagus sylvatica 82
Ficus carica 97
Fig 97
Fir, Caucasian 12
Common Silver 11
Grand 13
Noble 14
Foxglove-tree 180
Frangula alnus 161
Fraxinus excelsior 176
ornus 177

Ginkgo biloba 57
Gleditsia triacanthos 140
Golden-rain-tree 144
Guelder-rose 182
Gum, Cider 171
Snow 172
Sweet 100

Hamamelis mollis 99
Hawthorn 115
Midland 116
Hazel 80
Witch 99
Hemlock-Spruce, Eastern 22
Western 23
Hippophae rhamnoides 162
Holly 157
Highclere 158
Hornbeam 79
Horse-chestnut 154
Red 155

Ilex × altaclarensis 158
aquifolium 157

Judas-tree 141
Juglans regia 72
Juneberry 117
Juniper 54
Juniperus communis 54
virginiana 55

Koelreuteria paniculata 144

Laburnum 142
Voss's 143
Laburnum anagyroides 142
× *watereri* 143

Larch, European 36
Japanese 37
Larix decidua 36
kaempferi 37
Laurel, Cherry 136
Portugal 137
Laurus nobilis 98
Laurustinus 184
Lilac 178
Lime, Caucasian 167
Common 166
Large-leaved 168
Silver 169
Small-leaved 165
Weeping Silver 170
Liquidamber styraciflua 100
Liriodendron tulipifera 104
Locust, Honey 140

Magnolia, Evergreen 101
Magnolia grandiflora 101
Maidenhair-tree 57
Malus domestica 110
×*floribunda* 111
sylvestris 109
Maple, Field 152
Norway 148
Red 150
Silver 149
Smooth Japanese 151
Medlar 113
Mespilus germanica 113
Metasequoia glyptostroboides 42
Monkey Puzzle 46
Morus nigra 96
Mulberry, Black 96

Nothofagus obliqua 83

Oak, Evergreen 84
Lucombe 85
Pedunculate 88
Red 89
Scarlet 90
Sessile 87
Turkey 86
Osier 65

Palm, Chinese Windmill 186
Paulownia tomentosa 180
Peach 125
Pear, Common 105
Plymouth 108
Wild 106
Willow-leaved 107
Picea abies subsp. *abies* 15
breweriana 16
engelmannii 19
glauca 21
omorika 20
pungens 18
sitchensis 17
Pine, Austrian 29
Bhutan 35
Corsican 26
Dwarf Mountain 28
Macedonian 34
Maritime 30
Monterey 31
Scots 27
Shore 25
Western Yellow 28
Weymouth 29
Pinus contorta 25
mugo 28
nigra subsp. *laricio* 26
nigra subsp. *nigra* 29
peuce 34
pinaster 30
ponderosa 32
radiata 31

strobus 33
sylvestris 27
wallichiana 35
Plane, London 102
Oriental 103
Platanus × *hispanica* 102
orientalis 103
Plum, Cherry 127
Wild 129
Poplar, Black 70
Grey 68
Lombardy 71
White 67
Populus alba 67
× *canescens* 68
nigra 70
nigra var. *italica* 71
tremula 69
Prunus avium 132
cerasifera 127
cerasus 133
domestica 129
dulcis 126
laurocerasus 136
lusitanica 137
padus 134
persica 125
serotina 135
serrulata 130
spinosa 128
subhirtella 131
Pterocarya fraxinifolius 73
Pseudotsuga menzesii 24
Pyrus communis 105
cordata 108
pyraster 106
salicifolia 107

Quercus cerris 86
coccinea 90
ilex 84
petraea 87
× *pseudosuber* 85
robur 88
rubra 89
Quince 112

Redwood, Coast 43
Dawn 42
Rhamnus catharticus 160
Rhododendron 175
Rhododendron ponticum 175
Rhus typhina 146
Robinia pseudacacia 139
Rowan 119
Hupeh 120

Salix alba 61
caprea 64
cinerea 63
daphnoides 66
fragilis 60
pentandra 58
× *sepulcralis* 62
triandra 59
viminalis 65
Sambucus nigra 181
Sea-buckthorn 162
Service-tree, Bastard 121
True 118
Wild 122
Sequoia sempervirens 43
Sequoiadendron giganteum 44
Sorbus aria 124
aucuparia 119
domestica 118
hupehensis 120
hybrida 121
intermedia 123
torminalis 122

Spindle-tree 159
Spruce, Brewer's Weeping 16
  Colorado 18
  Engelmann's 19
  Norway 15
  Serbian 20
  Sitka 17
  White 21
Strawberry-tree 174
Sumach, Stag's-horn 146
Swamp-Cypress 41
Sycamore 147
Syringa vulgaris 178

Tamarisk 164
  African 163
Tamarix africana 163
  gallica 164
Taxodium distichum 41
Taxus baccata 56
Thuja plicata 47
Tilia cordata 165
  ×*euchlora* 167
  petiolaris 170
  platyphyllos 168
  tomentosa 169
  ×*vulgaris* 166
Trachycarpus fortunei 186
Tree-of-Heaven 145
Tsuga canadensis 22
  heterophylla 23
  glabra 91
  laevis 94
  minor 93
  procera 92
Tulip-tree 105

Viburnum lantana 183
  opulus 182
  tinus 184

Walnut 72
Wayfaring-tree 183
Wellingtonia 44
Whitebeam 124
  Swedish 123
Willow, Almond 59
  Bay 58
  Crack 60
  European Violet 66
  Goat 64
  Golden Weeping 62
  Grey 63
  Osier 65
  White 61
Wingnut, Caucasian 73

Yew 56

Zelkova carpinifolia 95

OTHER COLLINS WILD GUIDES

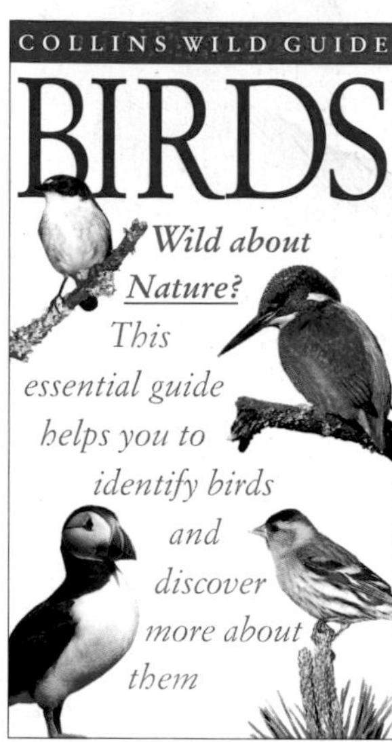
COLLINS WILD GUIDE
BIRDS
Wild about Nature? This essential guide helps you to identify birds and discover more about them

COLLINS WILD GUIDE
BUTTERFLIES & MOTHS
Wild about Nature? This essential guide helps you to identify butterflies & moths and discover more about them

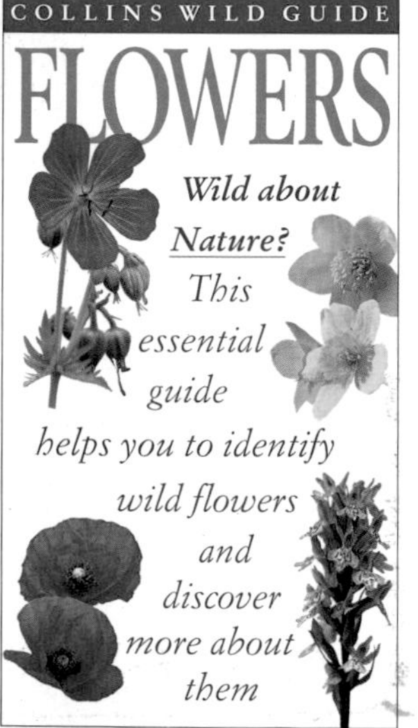
COLLINS WILD GUIDE
FLOWERS
Wild about Nature? This essential guide helps you to identify wild flowers and discover more about them

COLLINS WILD GUIDE
MUSHROOMS & TOADSTOOLS
Wild about Nature? This essential guide helps you to identify mushrooms & toadstools and discover more about them